# SPLASH!

## HOW WOMEN ENTREPRENEURS DIVE INTO SUCCESS

# BY LORIN BELLER BLAKE

FOREWORD BY MARCI SHIMOFF
BEST-SELLING AUTHOR OF *LOVE FOR NO REASON*
AND *HAPPY FOR NO REASON*

Big Fish NATION

Big Fish Publishing

Big Fish Publishing
1466 Santa Luisa Dr.
Solana Beach, CA 92075
*www.lorinbellerblake.com*

ISBN: 978-0-9769558-1-8

Library of Congress Control Number:  2011914202

Printed in the United States of America

## SIERRA, MY DAUGHTER.

You inspire me to be my best self every day.
You remind me that while I am on my journey
of accomplishing my big goals, I must stop and notice
the bugs on the walkway because, after all, this moment
is all we really have, and this moment is where life happens.
Always live fully, Sierra, and follow your bliss.
I love you with all my heart.

# TABLE OF CONTENTS

# FOREWORD
## BY MARCI SHIMOFF

Congratulations! You have just taken the first, most important step toward learning how you, as a woman business owner, can dive into success, by buying this book. Every page of *Splash!* reveals how you can envision, plan and achieve what my colleague, Lorin Beller Blake, calls "wild success," which looks quite different when you are a woman living in the 21st century!

The time is right for this book, and while it covers some of the same topics as other books geared to businesswomen, like goal setting or work-life balance, it is not the typical book you will find on these topics. Lorin begins by helping you discover and write your vision story, which leads you into determining and writing down your goals, with definite intentions – so integral to creating a life, both at work and at home, that is fulfilling, balanced, and successful in all the ways that truly matter.

In *Splash!*, Lorin offers up powerful nuggets of wisdom she has gained over the past decade, as she has interacted, coached, and empowered hundreds of other women business owners through her first book, *From Entrepreneur to Big Fish*, the Big Fish and Starfish business coaching programs offered through her company, Big Fish Nation, and her national speaking engagements and media appearances. While in the past we have tended to look at new things to *do* to create success, this book offers new ways of *being* that will create success from the inside and carry it over and out to the world. Our world is begging for ultimate responsibility. *Splash!* is about taking ultimate responsibility for our success in every part of our lives and what we are attracting to us. After getting to know Lorin when I was a guest on a radio show with her, we found out that we are both great believers in self responsibility – the idea that if you do not like how something is going in your life it is up to you to change it, to change either the thing that you are not happy about or how you are thinking about it. It takes clearing away our own glass ceilings, the world's pressures, the nine-to-five mentality, and our own closed mindedness, and then give ourselves permission to get a little crazy and start to think out of the box.

Lorin and I are also both big believers of the mind/body connection. Her energy is high and contagious and I believe she is on the cutting edge of what women need to hear next. She is the perfect person to write this book after being successful herself and designing a life that works for her. Her writing style is fun and easy to read, yet incorporates multi-layered concepts that you will find yourself thinking about and re-reading to gain their full impact.

While she includes quotes from the twenty-one women entrepreneurs she interviewed at the end of each chapter, and shares some of their comments throughout the book, you will want to be sure to read the interviews in their entirety on her website, *www.bigfishnation.com*. It is obvious that Lorin enjoys getting others to share their stories as much as we enjoy reading them. These women from varied backgrounds have shared their struggles and their successes concerning the wide range of businesses they own and operate, and will do much to inspire you to make your own big "splash" in the world.

It is obvious that Lorin has been pursuing personal and spiritual growth for the majority of her life, and I realized quickly that we are of the same mind, heart and passion. We are 21st century women saying we can do it all and still have a smile on our face at the end of the day. I want to do more swimming with this Big Fish and I feel confident that, after reading this book, you will also be ready to approach your business and your life with a new perspective – thinking not just of *doing*, but of *being*.

I am certain that if you follow the Big Fish lessons in this book and allow the successful women's stories to spur you on to do some things in new, more creative ways, you will find that *Splash!* will have you diving in, not only to "wild success" in the business world, but into being your ultimate *best self!*

• • •

*Marci Shimoff is best-selling author of* Love for No Reason *and* Happy for No Reason, *coauthor of* Chicken Soup for the Woman's Soul *and a featured teacher in* The Secret.

# INTRODUCTION

Welcome to *Splash! Women Entrepreneurs Dive in to Success*. This guide comes from real stories, real experiences, real successes and real failures along the way — not just from me, but from the hundreds and thousands of people I have had the opportunity to work with since 2001. I am constantly in deep gratitude to all of them.

First, I'd like to share my story. I am an entrepreneur at heart. I was laid off from my first job after college as a teen counselor. I was hearing rumors that my position was going to be cut because of lack of funding in the State programs. It was the early 90's. I asked my boss if this rumor was true and he assured me that my position was safe. When I found myself out of a job a week later, at first I was angry, but soon afterward I chose to look at things differently. I had been complaining about my job, hadn't I? So why not be happy about it? It was an opportunity.

It was at that moment that I decided I would be in charge of what I did to earn a living to provide value to the world. Very quickly, I knew that decision was truly one of the biggest gifts of my lifetime. Entrepreneurship has enabled me to feel free and fully responsible for my life, along with allowing me to lead my life with amazing flexibility.

After being let go from that job, I started a direct selling business. For three years, I worked hard, as I sought out the best training by folks such as Anthony Robbins, Dennis Waitley, Tom Peters, and Steven Covey, among others. After becoming one of the top five producers in the company, I quit the business. Why? It was time for the next big challenge.

I had learned great skills and was ready for the next experience. I also felt I could make more money doing something else. In 1993, I started an Internet company, along with a partner. This was when many people did not even know what the Internet was. We grew it to a $3 million dollar firm in six short years and sold the business to an entity that took it public.

I had the opportunity to be a part of the executive team while taking it through that transition and quickly knew that it was time to start something of my own again. Once I had the realization and confidence to know that whatever business I put my energy into, I could make a good and decent living, I was free. Isn't this what America is all about?

So, after giving notice to the acquiring firm, informing them that it was time for me to move on once again, I took a few months off. I spent the summer traveling to places I had not

LOAD

taken the time to explore, places that I had wanted to visit but had kept putting it off: Canada, Niagara Falls, Rhode Island beaches, and California. As I enjoyed my adventure I began asking myself, "What is my next calling?"

It was during this time of reflection that my light-bulb moment happened. I was a "typical" woman in the United States. I was just like your friend next door. I went to a small rural high school, a small state college, and my parents were divorced when I was in my teens. And yet I had been part of building a multimillion-dollar firm. It was then that I realized I wanted to support other women to create great success.

My next step was to become certified as a "coach." I had not known this was even a career choice. I hired one immediately for myself; thank God I had *that* good sense! From 2001 to 2003, I coached all types of entrepreneurs. As I found myself sharing wisdom, insights and inspiration, I realized coaching alone was not enough. I envisioned a company that educated and inspired entrepreneurs in larger groups and voila! – Big Fish Nation was born.

After all, doesn't everyone want to be a Big Fish? Big Fish like to swim together – to be in community with other Big Fish, like a nation or tribe. Big Fish Nation launched in 2004 and new groups of Big Fish have been launched almost quarterly since January of that year.

My wish for every person reading this book is to be able to do what you love and know inside yourself that you make the world a better place when you can count on yourself to follow through on commitments to yourself. When you learn this skill, you can accomplish anything.

That is why I've designed this book to be a guide and an inspiration— to take responsibility for being your best self and creating the most successful business and life you can imagine. Each chapter contains the following parts:

- The content
- Quotes from the interviews we did with 20+ amazing entrepreneurs who have created success in their world. Each of them is a "rock star" in their respective industries. Some you may know, others you may not, but if you were in their industry, most likely they would be your best competitors. They each took the time to share their stories, their real insights to success and how they got there. I am in deep gratitude to them for the windows they opened into their lives and minds. (All the interviews will be available online for you to read in their entirety.)

I believe we are entering a new world, a world where we will find increasing numbers of wildly successful women. The timing is perfect for an explosion in this sector of the world for many reasons.

First, we have to be in deep gratitude to all the women who have come before us for paving the way. Gloria Steinem immediately comes to mind when I think of women who were a part of the feminist movement in the 50's and 60's, and those who have championed our evolvement over the decades.

Then there is Oprah Winfrey, who is admired by so many for modeling for us what it is like to be human and have success. Through the creation of her television show, her related philanthropic efforts, and her new OWN television network, she has made a worldwide impact utilizing the power of the media. I personally love that she lets us into her world and is honest and authentic as she continues to evolve her business and, just as importantly, herself.

In the political arena, no matter your party affiliation, you cannot help but think of Hillary Clinton, who has endured, pioneered, and proven herself beyond the lines of gender. She has made and is continuing to make a huge impact as a female leader in what is still largely a man's world.

Secondly, the number of women business owners is at an all time high. A total of 10.1 million firms are owned by women (50% ownership or more), employing more than 13 million people, and generating $1.9 trillion in sales as of 2008. *(Source: Center for Women's Business Research)*

Thirdly, our world is in dire need of jobs. The economy is at an all time low since the Great Depression of the 1930's. While the times in which we are living may seem very imperfect and even chaotic, it is the perfect time to look forward and do what you love! As a matter of fact, in President Barack Obama's Inauguration Speech he closed with the following remarks:

> *"What is required of us now is a new era of responsibility-*
> *a recognition, on the part of every American, that we have*
> *duties to ourselves, our nation, and the world, duties that*

*we do not grudgingly accept but rather seize gladly, firm in the knowledge that there is nothing so satisfying to the spirit, so defining of our character, than giving our all to a difficult task."*

That difficult task might be starting a business that you have always wanted, or taking a current business to a whole new level that you know is possible but have not yet achieved. In these challenging economic times, I would also like to challenge women to grow their businesses to the point that they can hire that next person who supports them, whether it is an employee or an independent contractor part-time. Think about the impact it would have on our economy if every woman business owner – all 10.1 million of us – hired one part-time person!

Entrepreneurship is all about self-responsibility! It is about getting out of our comfort zones regularly and doing new things, talking to new people, and providing amazing services and products that impact the world in a way that we know we were born to do. It is about learning about ourselves and being more aware of our impact in the world. It is about learning about others, gaining wisdom from successful women who have gone before us and have already made a big splash in the world.

It is also about taking full responsibility for our happiness and making a choice to be "happy for no reason," as Marci Shimoff says in her book of the same name. And I believe it is also to be happy for all the amazing reasons that you have so powerfully taken responsibility for in your life.

Are you ready for a new era of responsibility?

We have visions to create, goals to set, and so much more to do in order to manifest big things in our lives and businesses. Read on! Start swimming, and prepare to make a big splash!

# CHAPTER 1
## THE BIG PICTURE: CREATING YOUR VISION

*"The greater danger for most of us is not that our aim is too high and we miss it, but that it is too low and we reach it."*
– Michelangelo Buonarroti, 1474-1564,
Italian Renaissance Painter and Sculptor

The first step to creating the life that you want, no matter where you are at this very moment, is to have a vision. You might be unhappy in every aspect of your life: create a vision. You might be so broke and behind in bills: create a vision. You might be living a life that looks like the perfect life from the outside and everyone around you thinks that you have it great, but inside you are miserable: create a vision.

What is a vision? It is creating a picture, written word, or image of the impact you know you can have in the world. A vision is a way you leave this world a better place than when you showed up in it. A vision is what you know deep down inside is possible for your life. Your vision is bigger than you are.

So many people are stuck in the past; they are looking out of the rear view mirror rather than the windshield. This is dangerous! Having a vision gives you something to focus on each day rather than looking back to the past.

> *"Fix your eyes forward on what you can do,*
> *not back on what you cannot change."*
> –Tom Clancy

So, how does one go about creating a vision? The process is quite simple.

First, take a few deep breaths, (some of us might need more than a few!) become present, put your feet on the ground, and find this moment. After all, this is all we really have. What does it take for you to stop? Notice your surroundings. Notice the people around you. Who are they? How are they? Notice your body. Notice how you feel inside. Notice your emotions. Notice your breathing. Slow down. What happens when we slow down? Some of us get sleepy, some go to sleep, some get excited, and some get distracted again from the moment. The only place to know and find your vision is from being present. Fully present.

Once we are able to be present, the next step is to notice what you are grateful for. Some of the things I'm grateful for include good heath, relationships, a world that changes, access to delicious food, the conveniences of our time, a child's laugh, a hug from someone who cares, amazing and genuine leaders in our country, a kiss from a puppy, sparkles on the snow, sunshine on the water, friends that call at the perfect time, a thoughtful message from the perfect person; the list is endless. Stop and notice what *you* are grateful for. Actually, write it down; make a list. You might be amazed at how much there really is to be grateful for. The best place to create a vision is from this place of gratitude.

Once we are present and in a state of gratitude, let's start with something that might seem odd or foreign to most. In your mind's eye, make yourself 20 years older than you are at this very moment. Imagine where you'd love for your life to be 20 years from today. If 20 years feels too far away, try 10 years. Let your body take you there…. *Feel* what it will be like 10 or 20 years from now.

Next, get out a piece of paper and begin to write about this image that you see. Writing does one of two things. It allows us to capture something we want to savor or let go of something we want to rid ourselves of, depending on the intention we have for writing. Whatever the intention, writing gets it out of our heads. In our head is not where we want keep things. We want to keep our mind free to work, free from clutter, and free from emotion. We want to keep it nimble and in good form, which allows us to use both sides of the brain more readily. We keep way too much in there. Think of your brain like a suitcase with two big compartments (left and right brain). By clearing the clutter, we allow both sides to function as they were intended.

The right side of the brain is creative, soulful, empathetic, and magical – the savior. The left side of the brain is analytical, practical, and critical – the saboteur. We need both. In business, thus far, many of us use much more of our left brain, but we are entering a new age. Daniel Pink discusses it in his book, *A Whole New Mind: Why Right-Brainers Will Rule the Future*. Business in this new age is going to begin to thrive as we become much more creative, much more into free thinking, less practical, and more creative. By freeing our brains from the details of life through writing things down, our brains are more relaxed. We are, therefore, able to be more creative and our ability to think outside the box is increased. This "outside the box" way of approaching business actually allows for more wild success.

So relax, breathe, and become present. Notice all that you have to be grateful for and when that list is exhausted, begin to write your vision story.

Remember that a vision story is just that: a story. It is all made up! But it is your vision of what you know deep inside is possible for your life. It is what you know you were put on this planet to do and how you will and can have influence. This story is *not* the "how" you will do it, it is the "where you are" and where the world is when you implement and use your life to influence the world. It is a snapshot of where you will be after 10 or 20 years of working and living in your most magical and impactful place.

Get out a piece of paper or better yet, open a blank journal. While reading this chapter, when you feel or begin to get a sense of your life 10 or 20 years from now, start writing.

Here are some questions that might help your writing flow. Choose 10 or 20 years, according to where you are in your life at the present time.

## 10 OR 20 YEARS FROM NOW:

- Where do you live?
- What is your home/space like?
- What is the temperature where you are?
- Where have you traveled?
- Where is your family?
- How are they?
- What is your mood?
- How do you spend your time?
- What kinds of foods are you eating?
- What makes you laugh?
- What is the tone of the day?
- What is the pace of the day?
- What are the smells in the air?
- Who is around you?
- What is the world like now?
- What is the impact you have had on the world?
- How does that segment of the world see you?
- What is different about you now?

- What types of sounds are around you?
- What do you see around you?
- Who is around you?

Add in any details that energize you. Let your mind be creative. Have fun with this exercise. Try to limit the vision to one page.

There are many reasons to have a vision. Everyone that completes this exercise thinks that it is for tomorrow, but it is truly an exercise that services us today. We will spend much more time on this on the following chapters. To reiterate, because it is a critical point, ***creating a vision is not for tomorrow, it is to help inform us today.***

As the process unfolds throughout this book, this statement will become more and more clear. The founder of one of our most successful Internet based companies says it quite succinctly:

*"If you think about the long term, then you can really make good life decisions that you won't regret later."*
– Jeffrey Bezos, Founder of Amazon.com

Remember that creating a vision for your life and your impact in the world is not set in stone. This vision document is meant to be changed, updated, and tweaked on a regular basis. It will change. It will evolve. It will morph. This quote by a famous musician says it best:

*"Map out your future, but do it in pencil."*
– Jon Bon Jovi, Musician, songwriter, and actor

When people write their vision, they often find themselves thinking, "How will I ever do this?" The how is not important at the moment; we'll get there. Rather, we want your vision to be so empowering, so inspiring to you, that you are excited to get started! When you write that vision, you listen more with the right side of your brain, not the left side that is always questioning if you can really accomplish anything.

The same thing has been said in the words of another:

*"When I dare to be powerful, to use my strength*
*in the service of my vision, then it becomes*
*less and less important whether I am afraid."*
– Audre Lord, Caribbean-American writer,
poet, and activist

So many times in our world, we see ourselves as victims or waste our time being angry, but when we have a vision, we step out of that unproductive mode and become our best selves. We become less hung up on the issues in our life and refocus on our vision, which has us more constantly in our *best self* mode.

*"People who consider themselves victims of their circumstances*
*will always remain victims unless they develop*
*a greater vision for their lives."*
– Stedman Graham, Speaker, Author and Educator

One of the best books I've ever read is *Man's Search for Meaning* by Viktor E. Frankl. Having a vision helps us find meaning in life – our lives and the lives of others. It helps us hold the world more sacred. When we have a vision we begin to see life as a resource to be taken care of rather than taken for granted.

*One must care about a world one will never see.*
– Bertrand Russell, Philosopher

The other reason for a vision for our lives is that without one we tend to wander all over the world. That is not to say this a bad thing. Wandering has its place in the journey, for sure. We find amazing and new things from wandering. But when we feel deep inside that there is something that is our job to do on this planet, and we identify it by writing it down, we tend to make decisions that keep us on a particular path, which more quickly takes us to our vision.

*"If you don't know where you are going,*
*you might wind up someplace else."*
– Yogi Berra

Another thing about vision is that it is not about reaching it! It is about moving toward it each day. Sometimes we miss it and sometimes we go way beyond it, but where would we be without the aim??

*"Aim for the moon...even if you miss,*
*you'll land amoungst the stars."*
– Unknown

There is another very important part of a vision that we have not yet discussed. It is commitment. Having a vision without a commitment to it virtually makes it null and void. It is just a possibility. Once a commitment has been made, something within us shifts. There are no options. Yes, the various ways of reaching it are many, but the end goal, the end vision is in stone. The essence of the vision has been written in indelible ink. This is an important ingredient when writing your vision. The details of the vision may change and vary, but the essence of it does not. The feeling of it does not change.

Commitment also gives us faith in the story and, more importantly, faith in ourselves. This ingredient tends not to be spoken of when it comes to creating and manifesting goals, but leaving it out would be a destructive mistake in the process. As you create and write your vision, be sure that it is something you are committed to, no matter what! There is no timeline in a vision. There are no "hows" in a vision. It is just the end image that you are committing to and having faith in.

> *"The secret of making something work in your lives is, first of all, the deep desire to make it work; then the faith [commitment] and belief that it can work; then to hold that clear definite vision in your consciousness and see it working out step by step, without one doubt or disbelief."*
> – Eileen Caddy, Spiritual teacher and New Age author

As you create your vision, be sure you are writing about what you *want*, not what you do not want. This puts energy on the appropriate aspects of what you want to create. For example, if you want to "create more joy and peace in the world," say that, rather than "stop focusing on the bad things that are happening in the world." Your words in this vision story matter. Choose them thoughtfully. If you are truly writing your own genuine vision (not your mother's, not your father's, not your spouse's, not your kids' – yours!), you will find this process enlightening, freeing, inspiring, energizing, and motivating. If you keep it fresh and read it often, it will continue to have an impact on your day – as long as you are making choices and taking daily action that moves you toward that vision.

*"The moment of enlightenment is when a person's dreams of possibilities become images of probabilities."*
– Vic Braden, Tennis instructor

VISION
QUOTES FROM INTERVIEWS

## Maria Bailey – BSM Media

"Women have to stop long enough to redefine what their vision is. I'll give you an example. Today, I had that momentary feeling like, 'Oh, my gosh, this is going to be the longest day of my life. I have flown all the way across the United States to stand up in front of 50 moms who are trying to grow their business.' But I have to tell you, when I got off the stage, as I was walking to the restroom, a mom told me, 'I have read every one of your books and you have inspired me to do this!' I had to stop for a minute and think, 'Okay, what is my purpose in doing my work?' And my purpose is empowering women. So, you know what? Did I do that today? Absolutely! And, I did it more for the lady who was walking to the restroom with me, but I did it for all 50 women."

## Lisa Druxman – Stroller Strides

"I think that so many moms, so many women in general, but especially moms, are so busy outputting, taking care of everything and everyone, doing all the things that need to get done, that they never get clear, quiet time to just be open. ... But I believe tremendously in the power of quiet. Whenever I am most overwhelmed and most overbooked I will take an entire day off, go with blank paper and nothing else – no phone, no email, no nothing – and sit at a park or look out at the ocean and expect nothing to happen and just sit. That open space, with nothing coming in, is where vision comes from for me. Some people feel like they don't have time for that. Well, to me, you don't have time *not* to."

## Julie Jumonville – UpSpring Baby

"My heart-of-hearts and what I've always wanted to do was to bring a product to life. I have had this green journal next to my bed and for the past fifteen years or so, I've saved product ideas of different things that I thought were either needed in the baby industry or in the engineering field. ... I've just always been someone that's catalogued ideas. I think I *did* have a vision within that notebook. ... I would stand on the rooftop or I would take out a billboard and encourage women to step across this internal line that they've drawn for themselves to follow their vision. When they do that, the stars align and success follows. You are happy personally, professionally, and that's when life really starts getting good."

## Lori Karmel – We Take the Cake

"I'd like to stress the importance of having a vision for your company. You have to have a vision on who your ideal customer is and I was the customer. Not everyone's business has themselves as their ideal customer but, other than visualizing where you want the business to be, you have to visualize who your ideal customer is: what they look like, where they shop, how they dress. You have to know everything about them and go where they are. You can't just open the door of your business and think people are going to come flocking over there. And when you can't visualize it, make it up, because that's what visualizing is.

## Jennifer Smith – Innovative Office Solutions

"I've had a vision and I've re-tweaked it and redesigned it.... So you've got to kind of re-invent as you are going along, and you got to have the foresight to see what the future might bring. As you are growing, the vision that you have out there might not be 100% complete. Somebody said this to me once: 'It could be like a piece of Swiss cheese, with all the holes in it, where you've got a vision, but you don't know exactly how you are going to get there.' You've got the underlying message of what you want to do, but you've got to have flexibility. Just look at the world today. Who would have predicted that we would be where we are right now? And I don't think that it's ever going to look the same again. So, you've got to be able to adapt to change and to be able to tweak your vision as you are going. Then you let your people help you design what that is going to look like."

## Mari Smith – Relationship Marketing Specialist

"When it comes to having a vision, it is one of the most crucial parts of your life's design, while also surrendering and letting go and never being attached to the form. I spent a whole lot of time writing this business plan, getting experience and training and applying for a small business loan, and thinking, 'Well, this is going to be my big enterprise based in Scotland.' But I wasn't really attached to that, and if I had been so stuck on the fact that it had to be in Scotland, I would have turned down an invitation to come to California."

## Cynthia McClain-Hill – Strategic Counsel PLC

"My vision is as much about who I want to be and the life I want to have as it is about the details of the work that I am doing. So, in thinking about who I wanted to be and the life I wanted to have, I then took stock of what my skill set was, what my relationships were, and where that intercepted with the road that I needed to be on to be who I wanted to be. That's how I determined what my practice emphasis was going to be and the kinds of clients that I'd be looking to acquire. The strategies for achieving those clients were all sort of built around what my endgame was and what my assets were at the time. … One of the things that I have learned in my life is that vision is a double-edged sword. It can both lift you and it can constrain you because you can become very focused on choosing the vision, and not fully appreciating that sometimes your vision just isn't big enough."

## Kendra Scott – Kendra Scott Design

"It was never okay to just be mediocre. I wasn't going to do this to be an 'okay' jewelry designer; I was going to be the best I could be. There was always a vision of greatness! Even from day one, I have always put out there in my mind kind of where I saw the company. We have what I call the Big Hairy Audacious Goal or BHAG…and it is to be an internationally recognized brand. We haven't quite achieved it yet, but I know it. I see it. I can almost touch it. It's there, within our grasp. We don't think small. We've always thought big and we wouldn't settle for just being okay. We are going to be great!"…

"A friend of mine, Cameron Herold, whose Canadian-based company is BackPocket COO, uses the term, 'The Painted Picture.' I think the idea, which basically is to write down your painted picture of where you want to be, is brilliant. We do this every two years. I'll write today's date and the date two years from now, and I'll write down every detail of where I want to be, where I want the company to be, where I see us, where I visualize how things are, and that painted picture is my map to get us there. I put the big picture out there and we've got it in our minds. This is the vision of what we want our blue sky to look like. We are all very unified here as a team and with my family. It's not just a painted picture of what I want here, but how I want to interpret that with the time I get to be with the boys and all of those things. So, I really enjoy doing that exercise and I love looking back two years because I've almost knocked down every single thing I wanted and it wasn't just stating goals. I looked back to my painted picture and to some of the things I didn't even think of. It's like, 'How could that even be possible?' Now, all of those things are happening."

# CHAPTER 2
## SETTING, WRITING AND ACHIEVING GOALS

Now that we have a vision for our lives that is bigger than we are, it is time to get out the pencils, erasers, white boards, magazines and scissors, or a blank piece of paper. This is when the fun really begins! Some people have actually never completed this process, while others tend to shy away from it, and others love it. The goal is to help outline a process that actually is so exciting that you enjoy it immensely!

There are, however, a few loose ends we need to tie up about vision that are not really appropriate to address during the actual writing of a vision. Now that you have written it, is it truly all finished and complete? No! It is a vision, which will change and ebb and flow and evolve. What does this mean? It means that your goals will change, too, but you have to have a destination!

So many people set goals before they create their vision. Vision comes first. *Without* a vision, goals tend to be all over the board. *With* a vision, you will be more committed to your goals. *With* a vision, you will boldly say "no" to other goals, and that is what you want! You cannot get to your vision without consciously and boldly saying "yes" or "no" to things in your life.

There is that fine balance between being 120% committed to your vision and knowing it is all made up – that place of holding it ever so gently, yet with full commitment. If you are in that place, you are ready to set goals. If you are not in that place, go back to your vision and write it so that you are 120% committed to it with the understanding that it is all made up! This is one of the paradoxes of success! It is knowing that you are committing to a vision and knowing that you made it up.

I remember when my daughter was born. I was 120% committed to her, knowing at the same time that she is her own person and will become exactly who *she* wants to be. This is very similar to your vision. This vision that you create is an entity in and of itself, bigger than you. It will take on a form all its own but not without your love, nurturing, and consistent attention.

Benjamin Mays was an American minister, educator, scholar, social activist, and the president of Morehouse College in Atlanta, Georgia. He was also a significant mentor to civil rights leader Martin Luther King Jr. and was among the most articulate and outspoken critics of segregation, before the rise of the modern civil rights movement in the United States. He said, "The tragedy in life doesn't lie in not reaching your goal. The tragedy lies in having no goal to reach."

While you are in the goal setting process, think of what is possible for you in your life, allow yourself to see it already accomplished, and most importantly, notice what it feels like to accomplish it. This feeling can be a great guide to you in the process, as it points to the intention to achieve it with ease. More on this when we discuss intentions.

The process of goal setting is easy. Always start with the end in mind, which is the vision, and remember that wherever a goal takes you, success is always there. If you reach the goal, it is a success. If you do not reach your goal, you *learn* from it. Always remember that this is a form of success. That being said, there is no "bad goal!"

It is critical to understand why we *write goals down*! In my first book, *From Entrepreneur to Big Fish: 7 Principles to Wild Success*, the first principle discussed is: Give Energy to That Which You Want to Grow. The bottom line is that the written word is a form of energy and taking the time to write is also a form of energy. By keeping the goal in our heads, it is limiting the various forms of energy we are giving the goal.

There are thousands of stories about how people magically reached their goals after writing them down. I am not suggesting that this is how it always happens; as a matter of fact it is not the norm, but it does happen! By writing them down, goals are given more energy. The writer gains clarity and there is now a medium to share our goals with others for support and feedback. So writing your goals down is the critical next step.

I love this example. Jim Carrey, the famous and successful actor, wanted to act and be paid handsomely for it, so he wrote himself a check for $20 million and kept it in his wallet. In 1996, he earned that amount for the movie, *The Cable Guy*. Now let's be very clear, he did not write the check and put it in his pocket and sit on the couch with his feet up eating bonbons. He was someone that intended to act, intended to get a lead role, and he worked at it. His intentions and actions were in alignment.

Are you ready to write down your goals? Let's dive in and learn how to use a goal-setting tool that will have big impact in your life and business!

Before we introduce it, I want to explain the parts of it:

## PART 1:
## 8 AREAS OF OUR LIVES

We set goals in *all* area of our lives. This naturally begins to create more work-life balance. At Big Fish Nation, we set goals in the following areas:

**Business:** What do you want to accomplish with your career and businesses in a non-monetary way? This can involve the impact you want to have on your niche, the products or services that you want to offer, where you might like to speak, or to whom, and for what purpose.

**Money:** What are your monetary goals, personally and professionally? How much do you want to make and how much you want to save? What are your gross profits; what are your net profits? I'd like you to keep this separate from your work … because it is! This is not just about how much money you make but also your relationship with it.

**Health:** Think of mind, body and spirit when you think about goals in this area of your life. This might include nutrition, exercise, and all types of self-care. You may have a goal to do some form of exercise five days a week, to limit red meat meals to once a week, or to book a massage twice a month.

**Environment:** I like to think of this as your physical environment, including: home, office, car, community, and even your world. You may set a goal to find someone to clean your home twice a month or to volunteer for a community beautification project.

**Significant other:** What are your goals for this particular relationship? Be sure that these are goals for *you* in this relationship; we cannot control others with our goals. Example: If you have a goal to become more intimate with your spouse, you cannot wait for him (or her) to be more intimate. Instead, you will need to take on the goal and be responsible for it. It is your goal! If you are not in a relationship, this section involves your relationship with yourself. Be the person you would be if you were in a relationship with the significant other of your dreams, and attract that person to you!

**Friends/Family:** Think of how you might want to spend time with family and friends, things you want to do, and how you want to be with them. Remember, the points above in the "significant other" area apply here, too. You can have goals but your goals are not their goals. If you want to create "we" goals, work on this area of your goals *with* your family and friends.

**Recreation:** This section refers to play! Some people think about how to play more – in other words, how to take more vacations and incorporate more fun activities into their lives. Those are excellent things to include, and the place that I would encourage you to explore is how to incorporate more play into every single day! Stretch yourself here; we are way too serious the majority of the time.

**Personal/Spiritual Growth:** Think about things you might want to do to grow in any and all areas. Goals might include books you want to read, classes you want to attend, and practices you want to incorporate into your daily life (i.e. daily prayer or meditation). You may want to set a goal to hire a coach or to be more present as a parent. Goals here can be anything to develop you personally and/or spiritually.

## PART 2:
## GOALS

A goal is defined by dictionary.com as "the end toward which effort is directed." Goals need to be:

- Specific
- Measurable and
- Time-targeted

For example:

- I will exercise 10 minutes per day.
- I will acknowledge my partner positively 3 times per day.
- I will complete writing content for my book by April 30th.
- I will launch our Big Fish Self Study program by June.
- I will attend a women's retreat for me by September.
- I will buy a new "green car" next year.
- I will increase my income by 25% by the end of this year.
- I will work on being in *best self* 90% of the time, one week at a time, rating myself at the end of the each week this year.
- I will enroll my daughter in swim classes this summer.
- I will spend 30 minutes of quality time with my daughter each day.
- I will hike one Adirondack Mountain with friends this year.
- I will speak with five (5) new potential Big Fish each week this year and keep track of each relationship in my new customer relationship management tool.
- I will speak publicly to audiences larger than 100 at least 20 times this year.

As you can see by the example list above, *some* goals are forever ongoing. In other words, we are trying to create a new lifestyle or business routine. We call these *daily habits*. Other goals are *one-time* goals that we can complete and check off. Both are goals and are very different. We need both kinds of goals to make significant changes in our lives and businesses.

It does not really matter what area your goals get into, it matters most that they get written down. We use these eight areas to help us think holistically about life, so don't worry about which goals go into which box. Focus instead on the fact that your goals feel as though they touch on all aspects of your life.

Begin to think about what you want to accomplish in a calendar year, no matter the time of year. This exercise can be done any time. Think about all aspects of your life as mentioned above.

Writing down your goals can be accomplished in any number of ways. Just begin by writing them down in a blank journal or on a piece of paper, adding magazine photos or in whatever way is most fun for you. At the end of this chapter, we will give you the one page plan that we use at Big Fish Nation. The key here, as you think of goals you want to achieve, is to capture them in any format that speaks to you.

Marc Allen, the author of *The Greatest Secret of All: Moving Beyond Abundance to a Life of True Fulfillment*, says it well, "The simple step of writing down your ideal scene can lead you to discover the unfailing natural laws of manifestation."

In the January 2009 issue of Real Simple, it was reported that 72% of women say happiness lies in making progress toward their goals, even if they never achieve them! Having a vision with a plan creates more joy. I have witnessed this hundreds of times over. I believe the reason this is true is because we begin working toward things that are bigger than ourselves. It gets our egos out of the way. We think less about ourselves and more about the impact we want to have, and how to help others in the world.

The other thing that I have witnessed is if this process is created out of pure joy and is aligned with the vision, the Universe begins to work with us. (Feel free to use your own word here: God, Creator, the World, etc.) I like to think of it as a process of "co-creation." We do not do it by ourselves and the Universe does not do it by itself; we co-create it. Putting goals and visions down on paper helps the world around us know what we want. It is a form of "asking." David S. Jordan, the most influential of all American ichthyologists, said: "The world steps aside to let any man pass if he knows where he is going." But first, it is our responsibility as a human on this planet to know where we are going.

When you read the stories of the women business owners we interviewed, that you may access on our website (*www. bigfishnation.com*), some of you might say, "They had it easy," or "Life just went their way." But they did their part. They knew where they were going. Knowing is a key ingredient. We tend to ignore the knowing inside of us. This is one of the important keys to success – listening to that knowing and taking action based on that knowing. Much more about this will be included in Chapter 3 – Intention and Intuition.

Once our goals are written down, it is critical to notice where we put our energy, what we focus on, and what we keep in our mind's eye. One of the women I interviewed for this book (Alyssa Bayer) explained that she has her annual goals with her at all times. She looks at her goals every day! This is a perfect example of the choice we have about where we put our energy.

She focuses her attention consistently on her goals. The result is that her thoughts and actions are consistently aligned with her goals. This is a unique skill that creates success!

Kathleen Norris, an American novelist (1880-1966) who was the highest-paid female writer of her time, said, "Before you begin a thing, remind yourself that difficulties and delays quite impossible to foresee are ahead. You can only see one thing clearly, and that is your goal. Form a mental vision of that and cling to it through thick and thin."

Earlier in this chapter, I spoke of commitment being a critical ingredient to your vision and that it is just as critical an ingredient to reaching your goals. Robert Conklin, teacher, author and speaker, says it well, "If you make the unconditional commitment to reach your most important goals, if the strength of your decision is sufficient, you will find the way and the power to achieve your goals." Too many times I see people that have a goal but with no commitment and this makes for lousy motivation to complete it. Many successful people will say, "There was not an option." They made the *decision* to accomplish the goal. There were no excuses. Nothing got in the way, or if it did, it was seen as a temporary hurdle to overcome, nothing more.

W. E. B. DuBois (1868-1963), civil rights activist and author, says it best, "There is in this world no such force as the force of a man determined to rise." The key word here is determined. When we are determined to reach a certain goal or accomplishment, nothing gets in our way for long. There is an energy that comes with that person that is unstoppable. You can tell by how they walk, how they talk, and how they carry themselves. We will discuss this in more detail in Chapter 5, which covers responsibility, choice and confidence.

The final point is that when we set goals we often think we need to do it all ourselves. This is especially true of women, but we do not need to do it alone. I love the signs on some of the ski slopes around the country that say: "Do not ski alone!" It is true here, too. Do not try to complete your goal alone! Wildly successful women ask for help! They delegate, they reach out, they identify goals and who might be able to help them, they ask those close to them and they also ask those they may not know but who have blazed the trail ahead of them.

Recently, I met a woman leader who was in the audience during one of my keynote speeches. Afterward, she told me she liked what she heard and said, "If there is any way I can help you, let me know." She offered her card and left it in my court. A few weeks later, I called her to ask if she'd be willing to do an interview for this book. She was happy to participate and after the interview she offered again to help. She taught me something about asking for help. Sometimes we ask for help when we are at our lowest, but really, the place to ask for help is when we are doing our best! (Thank you, Cynthia!)

So, once you complete the writing of your goals, revisit them through the lens of "who can help me." Begin to make a list of allies you can call upon along your journey. Ask them for help in a very specific way. Most of the time, you will find they want to help and would be happy to do so! Your journey to your vision should not be a lonely one, but one that is filled with an abundance of allies along the way. You'll find that you will, in turn, want to be allies with others on their journey.

*"Tell me, what is it you plan to do with*
*your one wild and precious life?"*
– Mary Oliver

# PART 3:
# INTENTIONS

A critical component of our goal setting process involves taking a look at what our intentions are while implementing our goals. Intention has been defined as "the state of a person's mind that directs his or her actions toward a specific object" or "a determination to act in a certain way."

For the purpose of helping set and achieve goals, I like to think of intention as a way of *being* in order to reach a goal. For example, if we are trying to reach our highest income yet, are we doing it with joy and vigor or stress and frustration? We all know that doing anything with more stress and frustration is nowhere near as much fun. It will take longer and make the process harder. If we approach the goal with joy, vigor, positive energy, and excitement, we naturally attract people to join us in the process. Intention matters. And, if we are more conscious of our intentions and our "way of being" to create our goals, we tend to do more great work, too!

In the chapter to follow, the concept of intention is explained fully and many examples are given. Your intentions should speak to you and help you in a way that guides you in how to *be* in that particular area of your life/work in order to create your goals. When we stay in that place and work on our goals, they are more apt to happen with ease. We all know people that set out to accomplish something big and make it look easy. It looks like no effort was expended; they say it and it happens like magic. It is all about their intent. Intent makes life easier and makes life fun.

As part of a women's retreat, I did the "fire walk," where I literally walked on hot fire coals, yet I did not burn my feet – not one tiny blister. This was because of the state in which I walked the fire. My state of mind was one that was high energy, with the intention only to walk and be safe, healthy and powerful. If I had worried about getting burned and looked down at the coals with fear, my intention would have been very different. My energy and intent were very conscious, causing successful results.

On the following page, you will see the goal-setting wheel that we use at Big Fish Nation. There are many ways to utilize this tool. I have it on the wall in my office and I look at it every day. I put a photo next to each section, as you can do on our iPhone application, Big Fish Goal Setting. I use it to check in and see if I am "on track" with how I am spending my time each day.

Some people spend a lot of time on it and then don't look at it all year, yet are so surprised at how much they actually accomplished at the end of the year. Others schedule monthly or quarterly meetings or retreats with themselves and take time to edit, update and realign "to do" lists with it. This is a very powerful way of utilizing the tool.

There is one more detail in the upper left hand corner of the goal chart that I want to draw your attention to. It is a place to put your annual intention. This gives you a focus for the year – a focus for an overall way of being that transforms you. Therefore, there are nine (9) intentions, one for each of the eight (8) areas, and one for the overall plan for a certain timeframe. We usually work within a calendar year for this project.

As you approach this exercise, always start with the end in mind: the vision that you want to reach. Do not start with the messy desk or the long "to do" list that has you on a hamster wheel each day. If you start here, you will get more of the same. If you start at the end, you may find some of that stuff on the desk might really belong in the trash!

Once you write down your goals, or as you are writing them, you need to consciously make a commitment to them. Have I said this before? Yes! It is so important to keep this uppermost in your mind: Goals *without* commitment are nothing. Goals *with* commitment you can take to the bank!

Next, you need to have faith in yourself to make them happen. You need to have faith in the world around you that the perfect things will come at the perfect time to manifest the goals. Be open to the flow. Sometimes, we want things in a certain time frame and they come much sooner or much later. Notice what you are attracting. This is a great clue as to what you are putting energy into. It also gives you feedback as to where to next focus your energy.

The purpose of having your goals written on one piece of paper is to give you focus. You want to keep your eyes on the goals and possibilities, not the obstacles and the fears that come up. You need to be aware of what you see in your mind's eye. Notice what your mind is giving attention to and know that you have a choice about that.

A reminder here: Goals are meant to be aimed for, but are not always meant to be reached. By aiming for them, you accomplish much! In doing so, you make major strides that you can both hang your hat on and learn from in order to keep going. If you think about any big goal that you have accomplished, wasn't it often true that difficulties tended to increase the nearer you approached the goal? When it seems the hardest, keep going!

Reaching goals is not always easy, but striving to reach them is an opportunity for personal growth. Many times I have set goals and not achieved them. However, what I did achieve was some new and improved learning from the experience that truly makes me wiser, more savvy, and more ready to dive into the next goal. Big Fish always find the silver lining and are grateful for it.

Achieving goals is truly hero's work.

*"We must walk consciously only part way toward our goal, and then leap in the dark to our success."*
– Henry David Thoreau

# GOAL WHEEL

**Annual Intention**

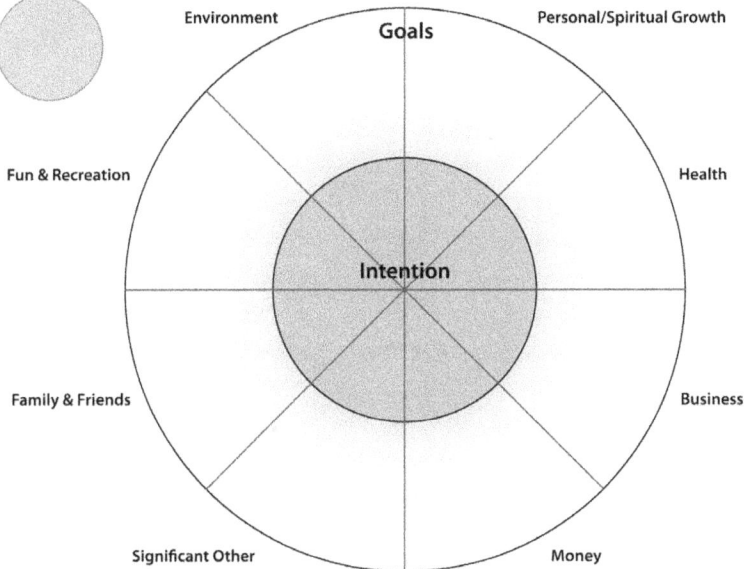

Goals

Intention

Environment

Personal/Spiritual Growth

Fun & Recreation

Health

Family & Friends

Business

Significant Other

Money

Current Year: _____

## NOTES: _____

_____

_____

_____

_____

_____

_____

_____

_____

# GOALS
## QUOTES FROM INTERVIEWS

### Maria Bailey – BSM Media

"My favorite quote actually came from a running magazine. I am a marathoner and the article said when you sign up for a marathon the first thing you should do is tell 10 of your best friends, because once you say it, particularly as a woman, you are not going to let people down, right? So, once you say it or write it, it becomes an intention and your actions and the energy that you put out all drive towards that goal. For me, I actually draw a picture of what the goal is, or I try to visualize it. When I visualize it, then I can achieve it."

### Alissa Bayer – Milk + Honey Spa

"I am a list keeper. ... I have a list that I carry around with me every day that has my yearlong goals and checklist. Every Sunday night, I kind of look back at my previous week's checklist and start looking at all of the important things I need to accomplish and when to accomplish them in the upcoming week. Each morning before I start my day, I review that and pick the few things for that day that I am going to be focusing on…but I certainly have enough time in most of my days where I can kind of go wherever my brain wants to take me that day. It's not that each day is completely regimented, but I have my five-year plan and my ten-year plan and I know what I want to accomplish this week and this month. … We all have the same amount of time in each day and it's really just how efficient you can become in making sure you are focusing your time on the important things that are going to propel you and get you closer to your goal."

## Maureen Borzacchiello – Creative Display Solutions

"I will sit down for business purposes in the fourth quarter and start looking strategically at what I want to accomplish for the following year. I actually have an annual goal: I bump it three years out and then I have five years out and I usually have an organizational chart that supports that from a staff standpoint. So that's how I start the process, and I just write it down: I commit it to paper. I don't necessarily develop a robust multi-page plan around that but I declare my intention of what my goal is going to be and put it in writing. I've learned to break them into digestible chunks because I tend to set pretty lofty goals, which can paralyze you! …. I may even break it down to what needs to be done or achieved weekly so that even if the monthly nut is a big nut it is more palatable."

## Elizabeth Browning – *BeWell.com*/Good Health Media

"My way of setting and achieving goals is I envision the future. Ghandi said, '…envision the future you want to create.' I envision things. So, number one, I am visual. Number two, I set goals. I am a constant goal setter. I'll sit down for this year and set down goals. Here are the goals for my company, three things; here are the goals for my family, three things; here are the goals for me personally, three things, and very specific things that I can achieve. Do I always achieve them? No. Like this year I am supposed to be losing ten pounds (laughing). The proverbial ten pounds have been on my list I think every year…"

### Kara Cenar – Partner, Bryan Cave LLP

"When I graduated law school, I was hired by this firm as an associate. It was a 13-attorney firm at the time and I think I was one of the first people they ever hired out of law school. I set a goal for myself when I chose to take a job there, as opposed to a larger firm, because it was a very family-oriented firm and I wanted to have kids. That was very important to me. So, I happened to get married literally three days after my last law school final. The goal I set for myself is I wanted to have all of my children by the time I was thirty and become partner by the time I was thirty. … I was thirty-two by the time I was done having them all. I have a nineteen-year-old, a seventeen-year-old, and a thirteen-year-old, and I made partner at thirty-one! So, I was close."

### Mari Smith – Relationship Marketing Specialist

"I do write goals but I am not as goal-oriented as some people might be. I set milestones. I am my hardest critic and I set these huge, high bars for myself. If I don't achieve them, then I get real hard on myself. When I worked for Harv, I loved how we used terms like 'minimum target' and 'extraordinary.' (I think the terms might be the work of Raymond Aaron, who was like the gold guru for decades.) So, you have his minimum, and you think, 'Okay...cool! I can achieve the minimum goal!' Then, there is 'extraordinary,' which is almost like that vision where it's just so outrageous that you just kind of let it go. But the fact is that you formulated it. You told The Universe, 'Yeah, it would be really cool if this happened. And then it is more likely to come to pass.'"

## Sandra Yancey – eWomen Network

"My goals are everything to me! I live for goals. My goals are tied to my dreams. I find that when you dream great dreams, they don't just come true, but they can just extend farther than you can ever imagine. I set lofty goals because I believe that it's easy to play it safe a lot. If you ask yourself, what do you think we can really achieve? Well, that's not a goal to me! That, to me, is just an expectation. What do we expect to achieve? So, I don't set expectations. I don't even like that word. Expectation is the slam dunk. I want to go beyond that. Somebody said, 'Reach for the moon. Even if you fall short, you'll land among the stars.'"

"I believe when you set great goals that they work in a couple of different ways. While you work on them, they work on you. You've got to be able to believe what you see, imagine the glory of the accomplishment, and also not beat yourself up. Also, enjoy where you are and know that you learned a lot, you stretched more, and you're in a far better place than had you just set expectations. Think about it. What word does expectations have within it? Expect. Well, you know, if that is what you expect, does that really stretch you? I don't think so."

# CHAPTER 3
## INTENTION AND INTUITION

Welcome to business in the twenty-first century! For possibly the first time in history, we are using these three words together: Business, Intention, and Intuition.

## INTENTION

We go into meetings for the sake of having a meeting. We travel to places because someone asked us to, but seldom do we ask, "What is our group intention, and what is our own intention for this meeting, conversation, or get-together?" Having an intention for the things we do changes everything.

Intention has been defined as: "The goal or purpose behind a specific action or set of actions."

Creating intention does a few things:

- Creates efficiency.
- Creates direction.
- Creates leadership.
- Creates a natural agenda.
- Creates awareness.

It also creates a time for *doing* or a time for *being*, but it is clear either way.

As a business tool, thinking about our "intention" for all that we are doing changes everything. I was recently speaking with a Big Fish who called a meeting with the owners of a competitor company because they were interested in purchasing her company. She had given them lots of information about her company, including its financials and structure. Her intuition was telling her that they needed to sit down and talk and she listened to that intuition. She called the meeting, but as the meeting date grew near, she became concerned. After exploring what her specific concerns were, we realized that while she used her intuition and asked for the meeting, she was stressed over it. She did not have an intention for the meeting, and she was worried about the direction it could take. After we discussed what she wanted her intention to be, immediately an agenda was created. Once she realized she was actually in charge of the meeting, her confidence returned.

Another great use of intention comes into play when we are writing. As business owners, we journal, we write out goals and we write business plans, but our intention for writing varies. For example, we might write journal entries about places we have been to savor the memories. We might journal about our challenges, in order to work through them. We might journal just to give ourselves space to be creative about our ideas. When it comes to utilizing writing as a business skill, intention is a critical ingredient.

Setting intentions as well as goals is extremely powerful. In the Big Fish program, we have been doing this for years. For example, if in business we have a number of goals but our overall intention is to be known as the expert within a certain niche market, our goals will bring us to that place. Having that intention will also tend to motivate us to be consistent in working on our goals, so the intention can do two things:

1) It can help us be the expert *now*.

2) It can motivate us to get to that end place.

The intention is an extremely powerful part of the goal-setting process. Turn back to the goal wheel included at the end of chapter 2. You will see in the diagram that there is a section labeled "Intention" for each of the eight (8) goal-setting areas. Here are some examples of intentions for various parts of our lives:

**Health:** To be "buff"

**Career/Business:** To be the expert in my niche

**Money:** To feel abundance

**Significant Other:** To be compassionate

**Family/Friends:** Connection

**Recreation:** Free to play

**Environment:** To be green

**Personal/Spiritual Growth:** To honor all

These are just some examples of intentions. They can be seen as goals as well but the difference is that they are all ways of *being* rather than things we can *do* and cross off the list. As we become conscious of how we want to *be*, our actions tend to change and we become more bold and consistent. They also have more meaning because there is a deeper intention behind actions that we are conscious of.

I believe that it is critical for us to have an intention set prior to going into a meeting. Sometimes it makes sense to share the intention; sometimes it does not. Remember the Big Fish that we discussed earlier? When she clarified her intention for setting the meeting in the first place, the agenda fell right into place.

We can also have intentions when it comes to family. I have an intention each day when I pick up my daughter from her half days at school *to connect* with her to find out about her time away. Each time I pick her up, my intention is *to connect*. I do not tell her that, but I am sure she gets a sense of that each day. I do not make or receive phone calls on our ride home. I do not listen to the radio. I only drive and interact with her. I ask her about her day and share a bit about mine. It is only ten to fifteen minutes of my day, but it is a time that I have carved out as sacred time to connect only with my daughter.

What I have noticed is if we have pre-set intentions for relationships we tend to reach the goal much more quickly and efficiently because there is nothing distracting us from that intention. Multitasking when we have an intention only delays the result and sometimes actually inhibits the intention! Single-mindedness is critical.

Another family-specific example that may be helpful is the following: Let's say that we have two families and both have different intentions each night at dinner. One family's intention is *connection* with each other. The other family's intention is to *eat*. Neither of these intentions is good or bad, but each intention will create a very different experience. The family who has the intention of *connection* will most likely be having meaningful conversation. They will be listening to each other's words. They will be asking curious questions like, "What did you do today?" "Did you enjoy it?" "Sounds like it was a challenge; how did you handle it?" While they are talking and sharing with each other, they will be eating the food in front of them, but most likely they will not discuss in detail the food, the weather, what is on TV, or be gossiping about someone else that is not at the table. The focus will be on each other.

On the other hand, the other family will be focusing strictly on the food and consuming it. There may not be much interaction with each other. They might discuss some basic topic of conversation to be polite while eating, but the conversation will be light and not focused on connecting. But, hey, they will have gotten the job done; plates will be clean!

If we observe the two families, without being able to hear the conversation, they might not look too different, but the outcome would be drastically different. So, we can have intentions for all aspects of our lives. This process raises consciousness.

Intentions are very simple to set. They can make a huge difference between a successful interaction and a non-successful interaction. Most leaders have intentions for most every interaction they will have. Successful women, specifically, tend to have an intention about each interaction. Here are a few examples:

### Prospective Client Interaction
The intention might be to be curious
and find out if we have a fit.

### Employee Interaction
The intention might be to inspire,
motivate, and empower to lead.

### Current Unhappy Client
The intention might be to listen to his/her
concerns and find ways to help.

### Current Happy Client
The intention might be to hear how our service
is helping and continue to support.

### Our Children
The intention might be to connect
and let them know we care.

### Our Spouses
The intention might be to connect and
let them know we are on the same team.

Why bother setting intentions? In greatly adverse situations, it is critical to have an intention. It keeps us on track. A few minutes into the conversation, ask yourself, "Am I getting what I intended?" If not, stop, take a deep breath, and take charge of the conversation with a powerful energy reset question that will be sure to be seen as a reset.

Setting an intention is not always about meeting your own needs; it may often be about identifying the needs of a group and making sure those needs get met. To clarify, I am not advocating ego-based intentions but rather intentions for the greater good. An ego-based intention would exclusively be about one person's needs without taking into consideration the others in the group.

If your intention is peace, this is only for the greater good of everyone. If an intention is to "get back at" someone or something, this intention is only ego serving. There is no win-win in such an intention. Pay attention to your own intentions and be sure that they are for the greater good or a win-win situation. Another intention may be to create fun and joy in the day, and who does not want that? If, however, your intention is to be heard but not to hear, that too is for your ego's good, and most likely will not lead to greater good. *Be sure your intention serves all in the group!*

If you set annual goals, try setting intentions to go along with those goals. (If you do not, I hope after reading this book, you will…) What you'll find is the intentions both keep you on track and also keep you focused on the end result you are aiming for. *Intentions act like bookends for your goals.*

Intentions may also act like bookends for a conversation. If you stay committed to your intention, you step into a more powerful way of being in the world. You tend not to let life drag you around but instead you tend to be a powerful leader in the world.

This is twenty-first century leadership!!

One of the women entrepreneurs we interviewed for this book, Mallika Chopra, tells a story about her father, Deepak Chopra, who asked her each night as a child what her intention was for the next day. What a powerful question to have our children begin to think about!

## INTUITION

The other business tool we have tended not to think about in business until now is intuition. While I believe that we are all using it – men and women alike – women are often less afraid to say that they use their intuition at work. As a matter of fact, they say it with confidence and pride.

One of the exceptions to this, however, includes my friend, Riz Virk, a businessman who has created amazing success in business many times over. He is the successful author of a book called *Zen Entrepreneurship*. He is young, consistent, compassionate, and very aware. After years of growing and selling a few successful businesses, he decided to put himself through business school at Stamford University.

Riz recently shared a story with a group of Big Fish Nation participants about a conversation he had with people in a Master's level class he was taking. The topic was how they make business decisions. As they spoke about testing, measuring, and researching, he pushed them to better understand the methodology behind the work. He said, "After doing the testing, measuring, and researching, when it comes down to a final decision, there is a moment when you ask yourself, how do I really take the plunge and go for it?" He continued, "When these business people finally got down to it, the answer was: 'Listen to my gut!'" You see, thanks to Riz, even at Stamford University they are talking about the power of our intuition when it comes to business.

Women use this skill almost without thinking about it. Therefore, wildly successful women tend to be quick on their feet. They make decisions quickly because there is less weighing of options over and over. They are able to be quiet enough to hear their intuition's whispers and are confident enough to listen to them.

So let's back up just for a moment to be sure we are all on the same page. Intuition has been defined as "the immediate cognition without use of conscious or rational processes" as well as, "a perspective insight gained by the use of this faculty."

This has been described for years as our sixth sense. Women are amazing at using their own intuition. As the number of women business owners has continued to grow over the past 25 years, it is not surprising to find that they are using their intuition in business, as well as in every aspect of their lives. Wildly successful women use their intuition every day, all day, and because of it are extremely efficient and effective in their decision-making. This is not to say that men do not; Riz is a great example of a man who has used his intuition extremely well over the years. But women seem to rely more heavily on their intuition at work and business — and it serves them well.

Here are two great quotes that speak to this topic from both the male and female perspective:

*"When I see danger, I step away. When I think
I can move forward, I move ahead, and when I think
I can come closer, I do. Sometimes I am wrong, but often,
if I pay attention, I am right, and these maps of my own
instincts guide me as surely as any Rand McNally would."*
— Mary Morris, British actress

*"Every time I've done something that doesn't feel right,
it's ended up not being right."*
— Mario Cuomo, Lawyer and former Governor of New York

So how do we develop this skill? First and foremost, let's break down the steps to using intuition.

**Step #1: Notice your intuition.** We need to be aware enough that we know we have intuition about something, and quiet enough to listen to it. Start to notice that you have many choices and how various choices feel inside your body. Play around with the various choices. Choose one and stand in that choice to see how it feels. Choose another. Stand in that choice and notice how *that* choice feels. So first, we must notice our intuition.

**Step #2: Acknowledge it.** We need to be aware enough to know to stop and hear the voice of our intuition and to acknowledge it. Noticing that we have this voice within us is critical, but sometimes we move so fast we do not even notice it. Slow down and notice there are feelings around choices. Stop and acknowledge the voice of our intuition. Know that there is not just the reasonable and rational voice but also the wise voice that desires to be heard. First *notice it* and then *acknowledge it*! Notice whether or not you are listening to it with validity.

**Step #3: Trust your intuition.** Trust yourself enough to take the action (or no action) on the issue or decision. This is probably the most difficult. Trust yourself and *act*. Dive in. *Notice. Acknowledge. Trust.*

I speak to so many women who get hung up on Step #1. Their intuition is speaking to them about something but they are ignoring it. They weigh a decision over and over and over again, wasting endless energy, time and resources. When we notice that we are spending lots of time and energy "thinking" about a decision, it is a great indicator that we are ignoring our intuition, and if we were to follow the three easy steps outlined above, we could have made a decision effectively and efficiently that would allow us to keep moving.

The other thing we often have a tendency to do is to act slowly rather than just listening to our intuition and acting when we really already *know*, especially if we think a certain decision should take a certain amount of time. For example, if we know what we want in a house and the first house we look at has every single feature that we have on our list, we tend to think we need to look at more – "just because." Our rational brain is saying, "This is one of the biggest purchases in my life. I want to be sure it is perfect," but how many times do we end up back at the first choice?

Bottom-line, intuition is a business tool of the twenty-first century and serves us amazingly well, should we choose to use it!

## INTENTION AND INTUITION
## QUOTES FROM INTERVIEWS

### Maria Bailey – BSM Media

"A few years ago, when Wayne Dyer came out with the book about intentions, I read the whole thing. It was actually a time when I was working really hard, but I wasn't making a lot of money and when I looked at it, I realized that that really wasn't my intention. My intention was the fulfillment part, the personal fulfillment, but I recognized that I did need to make money at what I was doing. So, I actually started keeping a file of proposals that are outstanding and the money that's coming in. It's kind of my cash flow file. I actually named that file *Intentions*. Every time I open it, it reminds me that although I do have personal fulfillment, I also have an intent to earn money and I have certain goals that I want to reach. I really believe that the energy you put out is the energy that you get back."

## Alissa Bayer – Milk + Honey Spa

"I think I rely on (intuition) heavily. At this point, my intuition hasn't done me wrong. I am highly aware of what's going on between the lines and things that are unspoken – how things are related that might not be fully apparent on the surface. I think the combination of me being able to read a financial statement and analyze something, looking at demographics and marketing and all of those numbers, and having that be in line with my gut check has been a good combination. While I have not necessarily gone against the numbers, there definitely have been times where things have first been intuitive. This spa was at first an intuitive thing and then I had to go in and prove it with the numbers. Right now, it's kind of the opposite. With this next project, the second salon, the numbers look really big, but I am trying to figure out how that will work with me and everything else that I am trying to accomplish."

## Mallika Chopra – *Intent.com*

"I grew up very much with intention as a driving force. It was something my father always talked to us about. He used to kind of have us state our intents every night before going to sleep. It was different from wishing or praying for anything, it's more just putting out these subtle intentions and planting the seeds that will grow and bloom over time. So, intent was always a big part. … I always think of intent as something like planting a seed of what you hope to aspire to be in the future in your life, and that would be personally, socially, globally, and spiritually. But I think intuition is more the way in which we make decisions as we then live our lives. So, intent is like planting that seed, but intuition is the process of how we feed and water the seed and give it some light."

## Lori Karmel – We Take the Cake

"Well, honestly, my goal-setting method is called, 'slide by the seat of my pants.' It is listening to your gut, which I learned is the most important thing. Sometimes an idea will pop in your head and if it haunts you and it just keeps coming back, you have to do it! When I don't pay attention, when I don't listen, I am sorry! One of the things that my gut was telling me was to get in touch with Whole Foods! I kept saying to my husband, 'I have to call Whole Foods.' He'd say, 'And say what?' And I'd say, 'I actually don't know! I just know that I have to get in touch with them.' … Then, I was able to get a meeting and they said, 'Well, what exactly are you proposing? Are you proposing that we sell your cakes?' and they came up with the whole thing. And I said, 'Yes!' The bottom line is we've been in Whole Foods for the Florida region, doing their sixteen stores for the past year and a half. It's been a very successful program. I just had a meeting with an ice cream chocolate shop that has about seventy locations nationally. I have this idea of cake and ice cream that I can't let go of. Well, out of the blue, one of the franchisees called me and she put it forward to the owner of this company and, right now, samples of cupcakes with a scoop of their ice creams in the middle are being driven to FedEx. I'd have to say one of the things that I became a believer in is what you put out into the Universe comes back."

"If you can think it, then you can do it!"

## Orit – Orit Design Group

"My gut is sometimes not so good, but it rules me. I think intuition has been a guiding force for me. I just feel something is right or I feel a person is right or I feel a design is right. Intuition is just feeling it. It's interesting because intuition sort of goes against that fear thing, because when you are so fearful you might question your intuitions, but I never did. I've just always kind of gone by my gut … I've been wrong a lot, too."

## Susan Packard – Scripps Networks Interactive

"I would say that women have great capacity for listening and they have a great capacity to read between the lines. If that's what intuition is, I think that we do an excellent job at those things. … I feel that I am a very engaged listener and I can connect dots pretty easily, especially around what the concerns, needs, goals, and dreams of people are. That helps me to be an effective manager. I do use those skills every day. … I think there is some degree of empathy that comes with intuition, which to me is a little bit of a mysterious word. But if you break it down, it's kind of how you can read situations and people and go from A to B when you don't have all of the information. I do think that women come by empathy very naturally, and to the degree to which you can have some degree of empathy, especially when you're working with people, I think you can be more successful."

"I think...you cannot go into a meeting without having a goal in mind. Let's say you are going into a board meeting. You need to know what you want to come out of that meeting with! If the board is an effective board, if you walk in and you haven't made things very clear, they'll say, 'What do you want of us? What's the purpose; what's the outcome that you want?' Nobody has time anymore, so you really have to be crystal clear. ... I know when I am going into larger meetings, I do a lot of self-rehearsal and role-playing of what could possibly be obstacles to my goal. How can I achieve my goal? How do I work around what could come up as an obstacle? Not only do you have to set what your goal is, but you need to be prepared to argue and fight for it."

### Jennifer Smith – Innovative Office Solutions

"I think that intuition and going with your gut plays a huge part in how I go about things in business. I might not know the answer, but I am going to go with my gut...and then you go with it!"

# CHAPTER 4
## CREATING A FULL, BALANCED LIFE
## (LIVING FULLY TODAY)

I have heard it hundreds of times over from women in all kinds of businesses: "I am afraid of success, because if I get too successful my family life will suffer." "I will not be able to balance it all." "I won't have the lifestyle that I have now." The truth, however, is to the contrary! In fact, the more successful we are, the more we can have the lifestyle we want!

For example, I want to pick my daughter up from school each day. I like to see the teacher for those twenty to thirty seconds at the end of the day. I want to hear how my daughter did in school from the adult in her life during the hours she is there. This is my choice. I want to be the one to have the daily conversation with her, to hear how school was, what she did, what she learned, and if she had a great day or a lousy day. To me, that is important time. It only takes me twenty to thirty minutes each day, but I would rather do that than make myself lunch. For me, the solution was to hire a nanny, who, in addition to caring for my daughter after school, makes me a healthy lunch. Then, when my daughter and I return, I can get back to my desk to work for the afternoon. Having a balanced life is doing what we love and creating a lifestyle and a support system to help us do the things that need to be done that we would rather not spend our time doing.

I believe that, unless you love doing it, you should not be cleaning your house! If you are an entrepreneur, you make more money doing your business (doing real work, not busy work!) if you hire someone to clean the house so that you can work.

Having a balanced life is really a bogus thing! There is no such thing as a balanced life. What is balanced to me may not be balanced to you. I move a mile a minute; it is my "New York nature." A balanced life is really about having the space to do all that you want over the course of time.

This may seem like I've made a sharp left turn here, but give me a minute. When my daughter was a baby, between one and two years old, she started to eat less of what I put in front of her and more of what she wanted. If I looked at what she ate for just one day, I would make myself crazy. It did not always seem "balanced," but if I looked at what she ate over the course of the week, she ate very well. I had to stop looking at the trees and look at the forest. Having a balanced life is sort of like that. We have to look at the big picture of our life.

If we go back and look at our goals and our goal wheel or the sections of our lives – Health, Personal/Spiritual growth, Career/Business, Money, Significant Other, Family/Friends, Recreation, and Environment – we cannot do something in every single category every day. On the other hand, if we look at a week, I am confident that we *can* touch on something in each category.

Creating a life like that is about choice. It is about having that greater vision for your life and beginning to create that today. It is about knowing your priorities. It is about getting clear on what to say "no" to and what to say "yes" to. When we say "yes" to one thing, we are also saying "no" to many other things. Creating a "balanced life" is about truly becoming CEO of your life.

As you create your vision, you'll begin to notice that your story has a tone to it. It might include words like relaxed, decadent, warm, friendly, calm, impactful, and healthy. Let's pretend that those words are used to describe your vision. You would want your lifestyle to begin to reflect that tone. This does not mean you do not work! This means you do your work in a way that has great impact. Why do we work 40 hours a week? Could it be because that is what the world tells us we need to do? But remember, you are in your own business! *You run the show!* You get to design the hours for your operation and for yourself! If you have employees, of course you want to be a role model, but you can also set up the fact that you are the owner and take great pride in being a part of your family's life at certain times. In no uncertain terms do we want others to be a victim of their lives. I think that our current world culture is so victim focused, we share how much we work, how awful it is, and we almost compete in our relationships. More work equals "bigger victim." *Mistake!* The goal here is to design a life that works for you. When we step out of the victim mentality, we step into our powerful *best self* mentality. It is the *only* place from which we can create the lifestyle that enables us to feel powerful, in charge, and balanced.

I believe we also have made a mistake in assuming that working 40, 50, 60, 70, or 80 hours equals how much money we will make! *This is not accurate!* There are many of us who work twenty to thirty hours and still make a full time income! I learned this the hard way. I used to work 80 plus hours a week in my old business. Now I work 25 percent of that and still make close to the same money. We have to change our paradigms, however, to do so.

The most successful people have found a creative way of working and making their work style work for them. It is not just about hours but it is truly how we choose to spend our hours that make for work-life balance to be attained, if there is such a thing.

What needs to be in place to achieve work-life balance? First and foremost, you need a vision, and the belief that you need to create a style of life that resembles that vision now... not 10 years from *now*. This balance issue that continues to come up has two parts to it. One is the *logistics* of being more balanced.

Here are some examples of some logistical things we can do to help us become more balanced:

1. **Quality time with family.** Choosing to pick up my daughter from school each day is one way I choose to have quality time with her every single day. So, choose quality time with family. It does not have to be long. A few minutes each day is invaluable.

2. **Book it!** I also put in my calendar my workout schedule on a weekly basis. That schedule is just as important as my work, if not more important! Schedule things that you typically let go by the wayside if you are committed to impact your life here.

3. **Daily goal review.** Look at your goals on a daily basis (or at least weekly) and be sure that, within your week, you create the time and space for each area of your life.

4. **Three goals per day.** Set only three goals each day taken from your goal sheet or "to do" list – no more. Meet your commitments to yourself (more on this later in the book). Accomplish those things early in the day and then allow the rest of your day to unfold naturally.

5. **Keep it simple!** People think that in order to have more fun and recreation in life it means more vacations! *Crazy!* What could you do every day for five minutes that is pure joy and fun for you? It might be to walk outside and notice the flowers, stop and really listen to the birds, or bring a massage therapist into the office every Friday for everyone that wants to partake. Bring fun and joy into every day,

rather than put it off for the next vacation! Bring a tiny bit of the feeling of vacation into your world today. It changes the feeling of the day.

6. **Acknowledge.** Take two minutes out of each day to acknowledge someone, either at home, at the office, or both. Doing this has us switch our energy to what we are truly happy about rather than things that frustrate us. Acknowledge those around you; it changes the tone of the day!

7. **Bold Actions.** Take a bold action every day toward a big goal. Progress makes us feel productive. It makes us feel that we are in a state of action and makes us feel in charge of our world. Bold actions are key to balance. Take a bold action in each area of your life on a regular basis.

8. **Health and Fitness.** Years ago, I was in the fitness industry. We (mistakenly) make people feel like workouts need to be an hour to an hour and a half long. This is really not true for basic good health. Dr. Mehmet Oz, cardiac surgeon and co-author of *YOU: The Owner's Manual* and *YOU: On a Diet* (among others), debunks some of the ideas we used to have about fitness, including:

- Increase your heart rate only 60 minutes per week! We need this for peace of mind anyway. That can translate to taking three (3) 20-minute power walks a week. Take the break to do this during work hours if you can. You need it!

- Walk 10,000 steps *daily*. (Wear a pedometer to see if you are close!) Park a few rows out in all parking lots. Take the stairs, not the elevator, and you'll quickly make headway toward reaching 10,000 steps.

- Work in only five minutes a day of stretch/flexibility exercises! (I do this with my daughter when she wants to get on the floor and play.)

• Incorporate strength training into your workout schedule. A total of 30 minutes per week is sufficient!

9. **Simplify!** Throw things away. Be clutter free. Messiness and accumulating "stuff" creates negative energy that truly leaves us feeling more heavy, more unbalanced, and adds to our "to do" list. I am a huge believer in creating clutter free space!

10. **Stop multi-tasking!** Yes. *Stop!* We think that this allows us to get more done. But really, it makes us crazy! Do one thing a time and do it well. Let's get more mindful about whatever the task is at hand. Love the task at hand. When we multi-task, we do not fully enjoy anything we are doing.

We can do this! Once we start to integrate these logistical things into our daily routines and burst out of our "boxed in" way of thinking, we quickly begin to experience a sense of freedom.

I think it is important that we know some of the facts of today's world, not to think of ourselves as victims but to understand why our fast pace really exists. In doing so, we can be more conscious and deliberate about truly managing our lives in a more balanced way.

The amount of information we receive today in one day is equal to what our grandparents received over the course of their lifetime. According to 2004 Census figures, 67 percent of working age couples are dual income, and that percentage has, no doubt, gone up since then. Both parents choose to work to support the lifestyle they want. When one person is not dedicated to the functioning of the household, there is more for all members of the household to do.

During the past 25 years, women's roles in the world have drastically changed. One of the women we interviewed, Elizabeth Browning, shared a story about her boss's response when she told him she was pregnant. "We are sure going to miss you," he said, assuming she was going to stay home with her new baby. In our 21st century world, we would never think to say such a thing because we believe and know that a woman *can absolutely* have a career or business and also be a mom.

However, women are making conscious choices so that we *can* do it all. Many are choosing to have fewer children; others are waiting until later in life to begin a family. Still others are finding creative ways to combine work and family through operation of a home-based business, or negotiation of flexible hours at their workplace.

Women are choosing to have a life where they *do* contribute to their family's income, their family's household, and the needs of the world. I believe this is as much out of choice as it is how the world is evolving. Women see themselves as having value for contributing in all areas. This is global progress! Michael Gerber, author of the *E-Myth Revisited*, says it well: "The difference between great people and everyone else is that great people create their lives actively, while everyone else is created by their lives, passively waiting to see where life takes them next. The difference between the two is the difference between living fully and just existing."

Women are choosing to do it all but, at the same time, are not becoming victims to the lifestyle that comes with it. We can do it all in a crazy and unbalanced sort of way (which is not really success, in my opinion) or we can find our unique ways of not following all the "rules of the world" in order to do it all. This allows us to be more powerful as individuals also. It allows us to be unique in our thinking so that when something is not working we can stop and think about a new approach to that situation. I believe that women see that we are in this world to contribute in a way that is unique to them, that is productive, and adds value to the world.

*"I am here to live out loud."*
– Emile Zola (1840-1902)

I believe we are all seeking our individual paths to "living out loud!" There is truly no other way, is there?

So many people complain to me that their "to do" list is *so* long! They go on and on about how much they have to do, and my response is always, "Congratulations, you are alive!" As long as we are alive we most likely will have some sort of "to do" list. It is, however, our choice to decide our relationship with it. Does *it* run you, or do you run *it*? What is your relationship with your "to do" list? Do you let it overwhelm you or do you see it as your vision in action?

I try to get very conscious about my "to do" list, only putting things on it that are aligned with my vision. In doing so, I find myself getting excited about all that is on it. I know that I cannot and do not have to do it all today. It is there just to remind me of things that I want to accomplish as I am on this journey to "the vision." Don't get me wrong! I prioritize, yet usually accomplish less than what I set out to do in a given time. At the same time, I try to allow my "to do" list to be just that – my guide for the day or the moment – and enjoy the task I said "yes" to that is currently at hand. Would I rather be bored? I cannot think of a time in my life that I was ever bored! There is always something to do, to be, to create, or to learn. There are always thoughts and ideas to entertain.

*"I never allow myself to be bored, because boredom is aging. If you live in the past you grow old, and dull, and dusty."*
– Marie Tempest (1864-1942) Entertainer

So, again I ask, "What is this thing called work-life balance anyway?" I believe the entire paradox of this issue is this: Slow down, be in the moment, and love what you are doing in this moment. Know that you have a list a mile long of other fun, great projects on your plate and, if you have things on your list that you do not want to do, give them to someone else who loves them! Live fully, right now, in this moment! Smile. Be happy. All we have is this moment. We keep talking about work-life balance, but bottom-line, it is about *doing a little bit regularly in all aspects of our lives consistently.* A chiropractor asked me a few years ago what I do for exercise. My response was that I am *consistently inconsistent*. What I meant by that was I *consistently* do something but I mix it up all the time. I walk, run, hike, bike ride, lift weights, rollerblade, ski, and on and on. That is life, isn't it? But the key word is *consistency*.

Bottom-line, work-life balance is about doing a little bit regularly in all aspects of our lives consistently. Consistency is really the only thing that has great impact on the work-life balance issue. Taking care of ourselves consistently has us feel as though we do take care of ourselves.

Abraham Lincoln once said, "…In the end, it's not the years in your life that count. It's the life in your years." We want to be sure that, every day, we have life in our days! After all, if we do not, we go to bed at night wondering when life is going to start.

Earlier in this chapter, I outlined two aspects to the work-life balance formula – *doing* and *being*. We have discussed the *doing*; things we can *do* differently. But I would be remiss if I neglected the other side of this issue. That includes the *being*, how we need to *be* in order to *achieve* balance. Here again, a paradox exists. We cannot *achieve* balance. We are living breathing beings, and we if we try to *do* balance without *being* balanced, we will never *achieve* it. So, the *being* portion of this formula is truly the secret to work-life balance. If we were in a yoga class but we constantly just did the movements or completed the poses without feeling or being more relaxed, we would not truly be doing yoga. It's the same with work-life balance. It is a state of being!

What does that *being* state look like? Here are some suggestions:

1. **Breathe.** Really breathe, deep down to your toes. Fill your entire chest cavity. If you actually put one hand on your chest and one on your belly, *both hands should move* if you are truly breathing.

2. **Slow down.** I find this one challenging, but when I get conscious enough to be aware of the silly speed at which I am moving, I breathe, slow down, and life magically changes!

3. **Notice our surroundings.** When I do the first two steps, I realize, "Ah, the wind is blowing, the chimes are singing, the water on the lake is calm, the sun is out, the air is warmer. When we do this, we begin to engage all our senses and, in doing so, life is more balanced.

4. **Acknowledge each other.** This was also part of the *doing* list, so that must mean it is ultra important! But acknowledgement is not just something to *do*; it is a way of *being*. When we get out of our own way enough to be able to see how others are being and what they are doing, we can acknowledge them. This actually starts with a way of being in order to do it well and consistently.

5. **Yes or no?** Be clear, conscious, and aware of "choice" in every single thing you are saying "yes" and "no" to. This guarantees that you will enjoy life more. It is when we fill our lives with "shoulds" that we begin to resent the world and ourselves.

6. **Be Silent.** Among the noisy world find silence. I notice silence at a red light. I notice silence after asking a question. I notice silence in a gaze. I notice silence while waiting for a plane. The world is a very, very noisy place. But if we actu-

ally look for the silence, it is everywhere. And in that silence, work-life balance is found.

> *"Go quietly amid the noise and haste and*
> *remember what peace there may be in silence…"*
> – From Desiderata, written by Max Ehrmann in the 1920's

7. **Be in the moment.** Moments matter. In work-life balance it is the moments that matter. My husband and I both work from home. Our lives are busy and fast-paced. Phones are ringing and we are constantly having our own conversations in our offices. Even so, we can sometimes walk past the other person, have our eyes meet, and say "hi" without saying anything. That is a moment. Or, there may be a time when he is on the phone and he reaches out and touches me when I know he is focused elsewhere. In that moment, he is letting me know I am noticed – and that matters. Create moments! This creates work-life balance. Creating moments does not take away from the time in your day and does not take any planning at all. It only takes thoughtfulness and care for humans in your world, and nothing more really matters. One more thing about moments: Don't only create them only when you feel good – create moments when you don't! You'll be surprised how it gets you out of your "funky mood."

8. **Be grateful.** As they say, create an attitude of gratitude. I remember that when my daughter was three years old, we began ending our day together asking, "What are you grateful for?" She was three and she got it! She would tell me two things she was grateful for and I shared mine with her. We have continued to do that and it is a fun way to

spend time at the end of the day. For an entire month, she told me she was grateful for the "puppy that JoJo gave me." Other days, she says: "I'm grateful for you, Mommy," and she gets to hear that I am grateful for her. She hears that I am grateful for others – for things we do, things we have, and experiences we create. I also tell her things I am grateful for about my work. I tell my colleagues in conversation what I am grateful for rather than finding something to complain about. It is amazing how it quickly changes the tone of the conversation! Try it!

9. **Be joyful about the little things.** We tend to skip over them but stop and be joyful about things that you are truly joyful about. Celebrate in that moment. This is much like gratitude but slightly different. It is about bringing joy back into your life consistently. I notice how many people don't laugh any more, and when something is funny we chuckle. Live out loud and *laugh* out loud!

10. **Reflect.** Notice your life. Notice your body. Notice. Notice. Notice. Be curious. It is amazing how much of life we miss and how much you'll see by just reflecting. It is the only way we see our progress, others' progress, and the world's progress. Reflect. Notice. Be curious.

This quote best summarizes my thoughts on work-life balance:

> *"The foolish man seeks happiness in the distance;*
> *the wise grows it under his feet.*
> – James Oppenheim

## WORK/LIFE BALANCE (LIVING FULLY)
## QUOTES FROM INTERVIEWS

### Maria Bailey – BSM Media

"One of my mentors said a long time ago, "The feeling of im-balance really comes when your priorities and your values are not aligned." So, for instance, if spending quality time with your family and your children, or going to church, or what-ever, is in your values, but then on your priority list for the day you have "clean out the garage," you'll start getting this feeling of imbalance. The reason you are feeling that is because your priorities are not aligned with your values. We are all driven from the inside and those two things have to be aligned or else your whole chemistry will be out of whack."

### Elizabeth Browning – *Be Well.com*/Good Health Media

"Today, we have Blackberries and cell phones and we're never 'off.' When I drive my car, I don't even play the radio. I just love the sound of silence. It is so rare, and I really need it, because I need to be able to think, so I think when I drive and I think whenever I ride my bike. I am a big cyclist and when I am outdoors doing any physical activity, I can really think. You've got to have that time!"

## Mallika Chopra – *Intent.com*

"A lot of my life is trying to balance being a mom and also taking on different projects that I feel strongly about. Ultimately, for me, the most important thing is my family. I see this with so many of my friends who are kind of in this quandary and all the struggling with should they be working, or should they not be working. There is always some sort of guilt about whatever they are doing. I think, for me, it's very important that I have always found that balance and being at home with my kids in the way that I want to be. ... I found someone who has now been with my family for seven years, and I can't even call her a nanny; she's more like another mom in our family, and she has provided a lot of stability. I have basically worked at home while she's been here. I have written my books and launched different things. Because of her, I feel like I have a sense of security. Plus, my mother is in town once a week, so I just have a great support network. ... I feel like the community that I have been able to develop around me – mostly women and caretakers – is really the reason that I have been able to do different things."

## Lisa Druxman – Stroller Strides

"Balance is something that we *all* have to work towards every single day. I sometimes feel hypocritical that I write on this and speak on this, because I can't tell you how many days that I don't have it together! I think that you will never feel perfectly balanced and so I kind of acknowledge that to take the pressure off the fact that you are never going to get everything done. Instead, again, pick from those little areas of your life – work, home, or whatever and say, 'What are the most important things in each area I can get done?' That ends up making me feel balanced!"

## Carla Falcone – Psi Bands

"I know for me personally, (taking care of myself) is huge! Because if I feel better mentally and physically, I am going to be in a better mood, more alert, more energetic, and more enthusiastic. It just affects my whole being. So for me it's just little things. Am I drinking enough water? I like really bright rooms and I've set up my office so that it's very bright. I have happy things all around me. I just recently created a vision board that is right next to my desk that I look at throughout the day, so that feeds my mental side. I get some form of exercise every day. Maybe I don't have time to go to the gym every day for an hour the way I used to but maybe it's running around and playing soccer in the back yard with the kids for twenty minutes or making some kind of fun adventure walk to the mailbox with the kids. I think it's just making sure that I am paying attention to my needs and wants."

## Julie Jumonville – UpSpring Baby

"I really do believe in spontaneity and I practice it with my children. My daughter is very structured like I am. I think that they are just born with it. The whole thought of her getting a 'tardy' at school just about sends her over the edge. So, I acted like I was taking her to school one Friday last summer and took her to the lake instead to go wakeboarding. It was just to say here's extra-special time with Mom, and a 'tardy' is not that big of a deal, because you have to have some flexibility. Structure is amazing and it really helps to be prepared, but at the same time you need to be able to handle and enjoy spontaneous things."

## Lori Karmel – We Take the Cake

"I have a 10-year-old son, and establishing work-life balance has been very challenging. We've had the business for more than six years, so he was four years old when we started it. I am very fortunate that my husband can help me out with this, but I hired really good staff and I have learned not just to delegate, but also to give them the power. They run the place. I give them that power and they know that I treat them as an equal and that I rely on them. I think the most important thing is knowing what your strengths and your weaknesses are. If you can hire people who have your weaknesses as their strengths, then you rely on them, and the result is they feel empowered. So, once you have that kind of staff in place, you can actually leave the business."

## Kara Cenar – Partner, Bryan Cave, LLP

"My first rule (about balance) is to embrace imbalance, because just when you think you have everything all in order and everything under control, somebody comes down with chicken pox! There's this stuff that happens that you can't control! And then you've got to figure out how to deal with it. I kind of look at work-life balance as a balloon filled with air, and there are going to be periods of time where it's just nice and and fully round and even, and it can float around. Then there will be other times where somebody's gripping one side of it and all the air pressure goes over to the other side of your life and there are other times where that lightens up and it eases back to the middle.

Maybe somebody grabs the balloon from the middle, and then there's pressure on two other ends, but it doesn't burst! You're always going to have something that occurs in your life. I have had extreme things that have gone on in my life that I look back on and chuckle about how I ever got through it."

## Cynthia McClain-Hill – Strategic Counsel PLC

"I don't know about that work-life balance thing! I don't know what that looks like. I've not achieved a work-life balance in the classic way that sometimes I think people talk about it. There is a lack of order in my life, but I do get everything done that I need to and want to get done, so I make decisions and I have been able to make it work. I have two kids and a husband who is also a busy working professional but we've had the same housekeeper for twenty years! And when I think of what it takes to raise our families… she's got two children now, too, and there's a lot of interdependence. We take care of each other and it works for us. … When people talk about work-life balance, I think, 'Well, gee, there are lots of things that have to get taken care of every day, no day looks like the day before, and you have the things that are important to you.' Are you achieving and doing and performing as you wish, with respect to these things? If the answer is yes, then how you get it done is how you get it done. … For me, it's like kind of looking at the entirety of what you are trying to achieve. Did you check the kids' homework? I mean, my kids faxed their homework to me when I was on the road! But we definitely dealt with homework and they traveled with us. My son is now nineteen and my daughter is twenty-three and I don't recall our ever going on vacation without our kids. So, for us, that was one of the ways in which we achieved balance. We worked like crazy, but we also would take a week or two and go skiing with the kids, because, gee, they didn't need to be in the first grade class. What were they going to learn? So, for us it was our own way of figuring it out. So, yes, yes, there is balance – not in a classic, organized fashion, but in a way that works for us."

## Sheri Schmelzer – Jibbitz

"It was very difficult for me to stop working when the business was in our house. … I had two young kids at home and one that came home at 11:30 a.m. I'm a stay-at-home mom and I was in the basement making Jibbitz. But of course I played with them and I did their thing. I fed them dinner and put them to bed and then I immediately went downstairs. I would get up early to see if I could get a whole bunch of stuff done before anybody else got up and, after three or four months of that, Rich actually had to pull me aside and sit me down. He said, 'Okay, we have to have a talk, because you are obsessed and you can't work like this.' …I was tired, but I was having so much fun! … I wasn't working out anymore or doing any of the stuff that you do for yourself. There was no balance. No more pedicures, no more girls' nights out. It wasn't because I thought, 'Oh, my God, I've got to go downstairs and work!' I wanted to! … I loved it, but I didn't know how to say there's time for motherhood and then there is time for work. And we really were outgrowing the basement. You couldn't even see the pool table. … So, that's when we moved out to this small office space. Then, we weren't even there for three months and it was too small. By that time we had five employees. Inventory kept coming in, because the orders kept coming in. It just wasn't enough space. Physically moving (the business) out of the house helped a lot (to get things back in balance), but then I also think it was Rich sitting me down and giving me a reality check. It was like, is this going to be your life? Do we need to get someone to take care of the kids or what's happening?"

"I think the biggest thing is just balancing the motherhood and businesswoman side of it all, and that it *can* be done. I have had girlfriends who tried to start a business and they could never define the business side and the family side and they gave up. I guess my message is, 'Yeah, it's really hard and it sucks sometimes, but I really, truly believe that you can have that balance and you can make it work.'

## Jennifer Smith – Innovative Office Solutions

"I have never liked the word balance. I think that my personality is that I am who I am, and I have the same values at home as I have here with the company. And so it blends together in a way, but it still all works. I really strongly believe that you work hard, but you have good time with your family, or whatever is important to you. You might not be married, but whatever your extracurricular activities are, you have to have time to do those things as well. If you are happy outside work, then you are going to be more productive in the work force, if you love what you do. I can be sitting at a hockey game and, in between periods, I can look at my Blackberry. It's not like I am going to shut off my whole work world and just concentrate over here. When people use the word balance, yet they try to separate the two, I say you just can't, and that's why I hate the word. You just make it work for you! And you know what? With technology and everything, it's so much easier now. Oh, my gosh! When my kids were little and I just had my daughter, and I would have to leave her at home, it was horrible trying to do it all! Now, today, with technology, there's so much you can do at home and be in constant contact with people if you need to be. You can get something on your Blackberry and you don't have to respond to it right away. You've got that choice, and if you need to respond, you do it, and if not, you put it away."

## Romy Taormina – Psi Bands

"Balance is probably our largest challenge because we both have children – young children – and so we are juggling quite a bit. But, I wouldn't have it any other way. My boys are in camp today. The camp is about forty minutes away from my home-based office, and to utilize my time most efficiently, I am sitting at this coffee shop having this conversation with you, knowing that I am really close to the boys should anything happen! I am available to them, first and foremost, but if it's not an emergency, I can get my work done during the day, whether they are in school or camp, and it's just trying to achieve that balance. I don't think anybody's ever going to do it necessarily one hundred percent, because we just can't be everything to everyone one hundred percent of the time. We have to be okay with that."

# CHAPTER 5
## A NEW AGE: RESPONSIBILITY, CHOICE AND CONFIDENCE

## RESPONSIBILITY

Successful women business owners know that they are responsible for creating success. No one else can create it for them. When we know that we are responsible for creating our own success, we see silver linings in every challenging situation. We see opportunity everywhere in the world. We know that if we create a mess – literally, figuratively or emotionally – we clean it up. People who are responsible do not blame others for their behavior – they own it 100%.

So how do we learn responsibility? It varies in every human. Here are just some examples. Recently, I was made aware of a program called *www.puppiesbehindbars.com*. This program is amazing. Puppies Behind Bars trains inmates to raise puppies to become service dogs for the disabled and explosive detection canines for law enforcement. The inmates learn to care for the dogs, train them, and then let them go. Each inmate is fully responsible for the dog during the training time, and through the process both the dog and the inmate are transformed. They learn what it is like to care for another living thing. They learn responsibility and with that they learn compassion. It is a program that transforms people.

Some of us learn responsibility because our parents taught us how to be responsible for making money, for doing what we say we will do, and for cleaning up after ourselves, so we learn various levels of responsibility.

When my daughter was three years old, she helped me learn one of the most amazing and simple ways to teach responsibility. When two children (or a group of children) at her Montessori school had a conflict, they pulled both (or all) parties aside and one held a "peace flower." The teacher asked each of them: "What is your part in the situation?" When finished, he or she would pass it to another child. Only the one holding the "peace flower" got to speak and share his or her part in the situation.

This can be applied to anything that happens in our world. We can ask ourselves, "What is our part?" If it is a world issue, perhaps it is that we are sitting back and doing nothing. Perhaps an apology is necessary to clean something up. We always have a part, no matter what the issue or situation. If you are reading this and thinking you do not, you are not being fully responsible.

I recently had the opportunity to hear Debbie Meyers speak. She is the inventor of *Green Bags* and sells millions of them on Home Shopping Network and in grocery stores across the country. She was complaining to herself one day about how many fruits and vegetables she threw away and thought, "*They* should develop something to stop food from rotting so quickly." As soon as the words came out of her mouth, she caught herself and asked, "Who is 'they?'" She realized, "They is *me*!" So, anytime you hear yourself saying that "*they*" should do this or that, you are really dismissing responsibility, opportunity and power that you have around a situation. If you are thinking that politics is not going the way you want it to go – get involved! If something at your company is not going the way you want it to go – get involved! If something in the world is not going the way you want it to go – get involved! If something in your life is not going the way you want it to go – get involved! Stop complaining as you watch the world go by. Do something! Take full responsibility.

I hear many people say that they want to make more money. Well, all those things in the world that "should" be developed or changed in the world are potential moneymakers someone is ignoring.

A colleague taught me years ago that a complaint is an unspoken request. Anytime you hear yourself or someone else complaining, you are shirking your responsibility to make life better for you and the world around you.

The beauty of teaching responsibility is that happiness tends to be the by-product. In other words, when we realize we are fully responsible, we realize if we are not happy we are the only ones responsible for making ourselves happy! So it is our responsibility to raise responsible humans on this planet. This in turn helps create peace as well!

For more on this topic, check out my Pledge of Responsibility Group on Facebook. It is free!

*"It is easy to dodge our responsibilities, but we cannot dodge the consequences of dodging our responsibilities."*
– Josiah Stamp (a British Civil Servant)

*"To err is human; to blame it on the other guy is even more human."*
– Bob Goddard, Author

*"I don't think of myself as a poor deprived ghetto girl who made good. I think of myself as somebody who from an early age knew I was responsible for myself, and I had to make good."*
– Oprah Winfrey

*"Hold yourself responsible for a higher standard than anybody else expects of you."*
– Henry Ward Beecher, 1813-1887, Preacher and Writer

*"One ought to examine himself for a very long time before thinking of condemning others."*
– Moliere (1622-1673) Actor and dramatist

*"Adulthood is defined by the willingness to accept*
*full responsibility for where you are in life;*
*no longer blaming others or circumstances."*
– Joe Westbrook, Networker and Student of Philosophy

## CHOICE

When we finally come to the realization that we are fully responsible and powerful humans, we realize that everything is a choice! If we love something, we know we chose it, and if we do not like something, we know that we also chose it, or that there is an opportunity to meet it with a fresh perspective, change it, or choose something else. Every day we choose so many things, from the clothes we put on, to how we earn money, with whom we spend time, what we eat, and how we respond to others. Choice is everywhere.

Recently, I saw a sign that said: "Life is not about waiting for the storm to pass, it is about learning to dance in the rain." This is a choice! We can complain about the weather or learn to dance in the rain; it's our choice!

This topic is so complex yet so simple. So many people say, "But I have no choice about (fill in the blank)." I disagree with that. We may not have choice about a situation but we have an *abundance* of choices about our *perspective* of a situation. All those perspectives are choices.

If you see yourself as a victim, you will have less choice. If you see yourself as a villain, you will have less choice. Even if you see yourself as a hero, you have less choice. The place that offers you the most choices is when you are being your *best self*, no matter what. From this grounded, calm, strong place, you are most powerful, most effective, most impactful and also most inspiring.

These perspectives that offer us less choice are perspectives that have us feeling small and acting small. At the same time, we are human, as I am reminded by one of my own personal coaches. He reminds me that, in this world as humans, we constantly run into situations that challenge us and offer opportunities to practice having more choice. Sometimes, I think we take life very seriously rather than sitting back and being an observer of our lives so that we can watch our own movies and then *decide* the next step rather than be *in* the movie and keep creating the same movie over and over again.

If we can see our own patterns we can then change them, but those patterns keep the fabric of our lives very much the same. Often, we want something different for ourselves. It is fully our responsibility to create the change we want for ourselves. No one else can do that for us.

We find that we often create the same relationships over and over again but with different people. Those people might include our significant relationships – spouses, bosses, children, or friends. It is not that those people are all the same. That is the irresponsible perspective that lets us off the hook. *We* are the only common denominator in all those repeat relationships! Therefore, this should be a great clue to us that we are the ones creating the dynamic. When we decide that *"they"* are causing the dynamic, we tend to move from person to person to change our world, only to find that we keep finding the same kind of people out there. The choice we have – the responsible choice – is to begin to take responsibility for our part in the relation-ship, and to give ourselves more choices in our response to these people. This is easier if we allow ourselves to be the observer of the relationship instead of the actress/actor.

Do you have a complaint about something? Ask yourself, what choice do I have around this situation? If you cannot change the situation, you can change your attitude toward it. Wayne Dyer says, "Change the way you look at things and the things you look at change."

Following are a couple other great quotes on this topic:

*"Destiny is no matter of chance. It is a matter of choice.*
*It is not a thing to be waited for, it is a thing to be achieved."*
– William Jennings Bryan, American politician

*"Every second, we choose to nourish ourselves in a way that*
*supports or depletes our lives, and to think and speak about*
*other people in a way that is honoring or dishonoring.*
*What choice are you going to make today?"*
– Gregg Braden, Author of The Divine Matrix

## CONFIDENCE

Over the years, thousands of people have come to me and said that what they wanted out of the Big Fish Nation program is more confidence. Many of these people are very genuine in their desire for this and they think that a program will give them this. Others will tell you that someone took away their confidence at some point in their life, but what is true is that we are the only ones who are truly responsible for either growing more confident or allowing it to be taken away. How many people do you know who were treated terribly by another human and are still confident in themselves? Millions!

So what *does* build your confidence? The answer is simple. It is keeping your word to yourself. It is telling yourself you are going to do something and *doing* it. The more we lie to ourselves, the more we lose or reduce our own self-esteem. The more we tell ourselves we are going to do something and follow through and do it, we increase our self esteem. It is knowing you can count on yourself. It is knowing that you can trust yourself. That is what confidence really is. It is trusting yourself to do something you set out to do, and how we grow that is to do something and see that we can do it.

A number of times over the years, I have heard Wayne Dyer speak. He tells a story about when his children are in a dilemma, his response is: "You know what to do." I believe that it is true about all of us. Deep down inside, we know what we need to do about any situation, and if we do not, it is a great opportunity to practice stepping out!

Let's say we want to lose weight, and we make a commitment to ourselves that this is the year, yet we do not follow through. What happens? We lose or reduce our self-confidence. If it happens again, we lose our self-confidence in this particular area of our life even more. This is true about every single aspect of our lives. Let's look at an example of each area. We just looked at the health area, so how about business?

Let's say we make a commitment to grow our business and we do not do it, year after year after year. We lose our confidence in this area and think we don't know how.

If we decide that we are going to create a better relationship with our money and we set out to begin saving and that does not happen, year after year, we feel there must be something the matter with us around the issue of money. So, again, we reduce our self-confidence in this area.

If we keep getting into the same kinds of destructive or negative relationships with significant others, we think there is either something the matter with them or ourselves, and we feel small in this area.

If we constantly surround ourselves with clutter, then clean it up only to create the same mess over and over again, we feel like we cannot keep our space organized, so we label ourselves disorganized or some other low energy term that has us feel less powerful.

In all these areas of our lives, we create patterns over and over. If we truly want to change our lives in one or more area, we feel that we need confidence to do so. It is not that we need confidence; we need a structure that has us build up our confidence. What is that? Simple. It is a system that has you create successes – big and small – on a consistent basis to help reinforce a new perspective that says, "Hey, I *am* pretty good at (fill in the blank)." Telling yourself that you will do something and then following through creates confidence! This is why having a coaching relationship is so powerful. The coach acts as a "confidence mirror" for us. We tend to look in the mirror and our "gremlins" rule. In the coaching relationship, our best self rules and the coach helps us practice this and break patterns that erode our self-confidence.

In over a decade of working with women business owners, I have seen that women who consciously work on building self-confidence *do* create more success for themselves. All our Big Fish programs are designed to build self-confidence and create a system for success.

The Big Fish team knows that we always have a choice around how we are with goals and achievements. If we follow through and achieve them, we build our confidence. If we do not, the "gift" is what we choose to learn from that failure. There is *always* opportunity! Over the years, I have worked with thousands of women business owners and sometimes I have found that the learning from the failure is more power-ful than the achievement of the goal! When we fail, we tend to beat ourselves up, and that, too, is a choice! We don't let other people beat us up, so why would we do it to ourselves?

Choice is in every moment of life, and the choices we make create our lives! Only we are responsible for our choices – no one else.

Some women say to me that they are afraid to create a more con-fident self, because they do not want to become cocky or "better than." I believe that in true self-confidence a sense of humility is created. What I am talking about is a strong self-image, not an over-developed ego! The two are very different! Self-confidence is practically a requirement for success, while an overbearing ego actually gets in the way of success. There is a humility that is present in true self-confidence that is not present in an over-developed ego. When we develop our self-confidence, we realize that the more we develop it, the more there is to learn and grow. It is the opposite with an over-developed ego. Often that person will say, "I know what I know and it is enough." The humility a self-confident person has is obvious; it is seen as clearly as their image in a mirror. They have a deep respect for others, a deep respect for life, as well as having respect for themselves.

As women are developing businesses big and small all over the world, we are beginning to see an amazing development. I was speaking with a woman recently who has done lots of work in Rwanda over the years. What she is seeing in that country is that, since the genocide, men have shut down and are not seeing the big possibilities in life as much. They are playing smaller roles overall. On the other hand, women are picking themselves up after being raped and being witnesses to murder after murder of those they love. They are able to push forward and hold close their dreams and visions of possibilities for themselves and the world in spite of the violence that they have endured. The women are emerging as leaders of that country and the world!

I recently read a book called *Left to Tell* by Immaculee Ilibagiza. Her story is amazing. She survived the Rwanda genocide by living in a bathroom for three months with seven other women. She spoke no English, yet took that time to study the Bible to learn the English language, because she knew if she survived she was heading to the United States. She is now in the United States working at the United Nations in New York City. Talk about developing self-confidence! Her presence is astounding; it is a beautiful combination of confidence and humility.

As you can see, there is a way of *being* that is emerging in order to *manifest* great things for yourself and the world. This way of *being* is present among most of the women that we interviewed for this book. I believe that this way of *being* evolves from developing a confident self versus the ego developed self.

One interview that we did for this book stands out in particular, in relation to the topic of confidence. Dr. M. Maitland DeLand, President and Medical Director of OncoLogics, Inc., related this story:

> "When I was made a fellow of the American College of Radiology, I had somebody look at my name tag, see where I was from, and say, 'Well, who would have made you a Fellow? You're from Louisiana. You're not from someplace that does great research or somebody....' And what I like to tell people is that everybody comes to a room in a different way. You might come through the front door, you might come through the back door, you might come through the window, but everybody's in the same room and that's when you can show your capabilities. Typically, when I do an accreditation, and maybe somebody thinks because I'm not from an Ivy League School that maybe I am not going to find something, I'll walk in there and say, 'Why did you treat this hip prosthesis and subtract the monitor units?' Well, immediately they know I know what

I am doing. So, if you want to take a risk and you want to have people understand what you can do, you need to show them. Sometimes, like I said, 'You're not going to be led through the front door, but once you get in that room…everybody's equal.'"

Some quotes on this topic:

*"I gain strength, courage and confidence by every experience in which I must stop and look fear in the face… I say to myself, I've lived through this and can take the next thing that comes along."*
– Eleanor Roosevelt

*"Always hold your head up, but be careful to keep your nose at a friendly level."*
– Max L. Forman

*"Take a day to heal from the lies you've told yourself and the ones that have been told to you."*
– Maya Angelou, Poet

When speaking with successful, self-confident women, additional qualities, such as gratitude, giving, and a lifelong zest for learning become immediately evident. The first is how grateful they are for everything and everyone. They seem to easily and naturally find silver linings. When they are grateful, they share that thought simply in an act, an email, a card, or a phone call. This, in and of itself, has them slow down in life and enjoy moments, so that balance naturally gets created.

From that gratitude, they regularly give to others. It may not be just in material terms; often it is not. But more valuable than that, it is in giving of their time, or their expertise. So often you see that successful women have developed a not-for-profit entity that allows them to give through that organization in ways that are above and beyond their businesses. Some examples include Sandra Yancey, with her eWomen Network Foundation; Sara Blakely, with her Sara Blakely Foundation; and, of course, Oprah Winfrey, with her Angel Network, just to name a few. Giving is a part of a woman's nature. It is part of her fabric, and successful women find a way to integrate it naturally.

Dr. DeLand of OncoLogics also exemplifies this spirit of giving: "When somebody comes in and they have cancer and are referred, whether it's a charity patient, a Blue Cross patient or a Medicare patient, everyone is treated the same in my office. So, I don't really know (if they have insurance coverage). I can have a patient that may have lost her insurance and I won't know that as a doctor. Sometimes they won't bring that up. Yesterday, I had somebody who didn't show up for her checkup and I said, "She really needs to come in." My nurse said, "Well, she lost her insurance." And I said, "Well, I'm still going to take care of her. She needs to have her check-up!" So, I think that's a very small thing to do. A person comes in and they are treated, and if it's a horribly expensive stereotactic treatment, it doesn't matter if it was free or if they had insurance; it just doesn't matter. You do the right thing and you do what that person needs. ... I don't even know if I get paid! It just doesn't matter because I want the treatment to be correct!"

Finally, successful women are constantly putting themselves in positions and places to learn. As stated earlier, a self-confident person *chooses* to learn and grow.

This *way of being* is very powerful. It is about having that *way of being* consistently in order to become who you want to be in the world. Of course, we are human, so we do not always maintain that way of being. That is where the learning opportunities are. But successful women are conscious about their way of being, in that it has them be authentic, impactful, and also being their best selves. In that place, their intentions are genuine and they have impact that they choose consciously.

> *"When you are grateful, when you can see what you have,*
> *you unlock blessings to flow into your life."*
> – Suze Orman, Financial advisor/author

> *"Silent gratitude isn't much good to anyone."*
> – Gladys Browyn Stern, Author

## RESPONSIBILITY, CHOICE AND CONFIDENCE
## QUOTES FROM INTERVIEWS

### Alissa Bayer – Milk + Honey Spa

"I have always had sort of an inner confidence. ... I have just had a really strong, supportive family. ... Having that level of support has allowed me to make a lot of the decisions I've made and take on some of the risk that I have. I think to myself, 'What is the worst thing that could possibly happen?' If this were to fail, as long as I have my husband and my dog and my family, I don't really care if I am in a studio apartment, because I know I will be able to rebuild whatever I have lost. My worst-case scenario for doing all of this is really not all that terrible, but the upside is tremendous."

### Maureen Borzacchiello – Creative Display Solutions

"The reality is that if you want to accomplish something great you do have to work at it, and I've always been willing to pay my dues from a time standpoint. I think that at the end of the day the most important thing is having confidence in yourself. If you don't believe in yourself, why should anyone else?"

## Elizabeth Browning – *BeWell.com*/Good Health Media

"It's responsible to be transparent to your people, so they know where the company is and can make decisions for themselves. ...Responsibility is key! It always starts with you and you set the example. As a leader, you have to keep the hope alive. You have to keep the vision, because once you succumb to fear it's so easy to just give up, and you really can't do that. I don't know that I've ever really been afraid of anything. There are some things that I don't like and situations I prefer not to be in, but I don't think that there is anything that I genuinely fear. And, you have to ask yourself, what's the worst thing that can happen? ... Life is messy sometimes, but we all come together and we figure it out."

## Kara Cenar – Partner, Bryan Cave LLP

"The way I see it, every ordinary person is extraordinary if they would let themselves be."

## Lisa Druxman – Stroller Strides

"Whenever I speak to aspiring 'mompreneurs' or entrepreneurs, I find that their biggest hold back is risk. They don't want to risk their home. They don't want to risk whatever stability they have. I say, 'Just take that leap!' Because I don't want to lose my home either, yet at the same time I realize no matter what happens we'll figure it out. We'll pick ourselves back up. So, when you finally release that, when you say, 'What's the worst that can happen?' the world's at your feet."

## Lori Karmel – We Take the Cake

"I think a lot of women fall into a trap of feeling like they are waiting for someone to come save them. They'll say, 'I'll just dabble in this, and if it doesn't work out, I'll get married,' or try something else, whatever the case may be. And, I would say to myself, 'I am responsible for myself.' My husband and I were going through some rough times after we moved here, because his business, due to circumstances, was almost nonexistent and we really didn't have an income, and the business was taking a lot of money. So, I really didn't have him to rely on. I had no money coming from anywhere else. And I just kept saying, 'I am responsible for myself!' Stop thinking you can fall back on someone, because you can't! And the follow-up to that is, 'There is no option for failure!' Make it work!"

## Cynthia McClain-Hill – Strategic Counsel PLC

"The one thing that I reinforce with people is the importance of having their own individual sort of accountability. When I was no longer employed, I had to really be able to move forward based on what people thought about me – on my professional reputation. So often we get caught up in companies or brands, whether it is our own business or someone else's business, and it's very easy to lose sight of what that company or brand translates to. What it comes down to is, "Do people trust you?" It's all about that relationship. What do people think of you? Are you accountable? Are you reliable? Are you exceptional? If you are willing to be exceptional, everything else will work out."

## Orit – Orit Design Group

"I think that confidence takes on different meanings to different people. I think that in the case of women business owners you sometimes have women who are really strong and quite aggressive but show no personality. They feel like that's what they have to do. You then have people that have the personality but, when questioned, they kind of shy away a little and back down. Then you have the women who are very confident because they are very attractive and they've always been the cheerleader, the class president, or the sorority queen. Their confidence comes from their looks and they've never really had to deal with the other part of it. So, confidence means different things to different people. I think that to me, confidence certainly comes from maturity and having experienced it. I think that I was very insecure but no one knew it. I always came across as very confident because I knew I was a good designer and because that's what I was selling, I was able to kind of wrap my arms around it and be confident about that. Not until lately did I realize that my personality and just who I am as a person was really what was driving a lot of it. I never came off as being overly confident."

## Susan Packard – Scripps Networks Interactive

"I agree that we are accountable for our own confidence. I could just call it being comfortable in my own skin, knowing what I am good at, knowing what I am not so good at, and being clear on what that is. Having said that, having mentored so many women in my life, I've seen that lack of confidence is a very recurring theme. We are not close to having women at the point where they need to be. I think there still needs to be quite a bit of counseling and mentoring of women in this area. We'll eventually get there, but it's one area that's been slow to come by."

### Sheri Schmelzer – Jibbitz

"I think that (starting the Jibbitz business) gave me self-confidence, which I never really felt like I had enough of. I had as much as I needed to be a stay-at-home-mom, with a marriage and family therapy degree by the way, and then, all of a sudden, within months, I was in the circle of executives for Crocs™. It was just overwhelming and I was scared to death! That's the part where I discovered, 'You know what? I *can* do this. I am *going* to do this.' My first big interview was on Oprah! To walk out on that stage, I needed oxygen! So I think that one of the main things that I carried away from this whole experience was a deeper sense of self-confidence, to the point that now I can say, 'You know what? If you want me to go into a room filled with Bill Gates types, well, okay…I can do that.'"

### Jennifer Smith – Innovative Office Solutions

"You aren't going to make every decision correctly, but don't be afraid of that. Take responsibility if you've made a mistake, own up to it, and you'll see that people will say, 'Okay. You are human, too, and thanks for being honest.' They have more respect for you."

### Mari Smith – Relationship Marketing Strategist

"One of the seminars that I did years ago included an exercise that really brings home responsibility and how most people think of it as kind of a burden. It feels heavy on our shoulders, but I love to think about responsibility from a place of joy, rather than as a burden. Because at the time that we are talking today, Lorin, I have 46,000 followers on Twitter, and

I know I can communicate to them in the click of one button. In 140 characters or less, I can communicate a message to them. I have a tremendous responsibility to communicate that message to them in a way that uplifts their spirit, and that contributes to the greater whole."

## Sandra Yancey – eWomen Network

"I don't want any employee that I am better than. I try now to hire employees who are either smarter than me when I hire them, or I know all I have to do is provide some coaching and the environment and support and they'll blow me away! Because if you are the smartest tool in the toolbox, I believe you are setting yourself up, unnecessarily, for some real pain and struggles, if not, bankruptcy!"

# CHAPTER 6
# MEN, WHAT DO THEY HAVE TO DO WITH IT? EVERYTHING!

This chapter might seem a bit out of place; however, I think that it is important to acknowledge why we need to credit men with the level of success that women are achieving in the 21st century. We need to acknowledge how men have supported women in getting to places of power and success, while being very thoughtful, conscious and strategic about how to take our businesses to the next level. We are not trying to duplicate how men have traditionally done business, because we actually think very differently about life and business, and our responsibilities are different as well. But men are undeniably playing important, even essential roles in contributing to our ability to integrate a thriving business and family life – that work-life balance we all strive to have.

So many of the women that we interviewed, almost 95 percent, spoke about the fact that their husbands/partners were *extremely* supportive of their success. Almost all of the husbands were supportive at home in caring for the children, doing anything and everything for the kids in a family where Mom is an entrepreneur. Generally, it seemed that there were no lines drawn as to where the spouses would stop to support the family. Many of them were cooking, cleaning, shuttling the kids, and "holding down the fort," so to speak, while Mom was out working her business, sometimes traveling for weeks at a time, and other times just with long days, day after day.

But most importantly, almost all the women we interviewed mentioned that their partners were emotionally supportive, and we all know that kind of support is what makes the difference at the end of a challenging day. Many felt that their husbands/partners were the emotional support that they needed to keep going. They spoke of their husbands/partners as their cheerleaders, their confidants, and their inspiration when things got tough or tough decisions had to be made. Many of the women felt that their partners/husbands/spouses "had their backs" when they needed it. Many suggested that they took more risks because of that support.

It is critical to have the support of a partner/spouse/significant other when working on creating a vision that you know is possible. It makes all the difference when one other person believes in your vision and your potential to have the impact you know you can have in the world.

Just recently, I sat next to a man on an airplane, a husband of a woman business owner. We were chatting about this topic and his exact words were, "Parenting is a give and take. I take the home responsibility sometimes and then she does." He even went on to explain that they take turns when their 3-year-old son is sick. He'll take the first day and she'll do the next.

The second critical point here is that men have been the breadwinners for centuries. They have been the ones who have been "bringing home the bacon," until now... The numbers are shifting and women now make up just over 51% of the workforce. As women entrepreneurs, men have also taught us, in some ways, how we cannot do our businesses if we want to have it all. Generally speaking, women entrepreneurs still have a great impact in the home as well as in their businesses, much more so than men have when they have a full time job. Women tend to work very different hours of the workday.

For example, they work just after the kids go to school and they stop working to be home with the kids for dinner and after the kids are back in bed, they are back online, getting more work done before retiring for the night. A nine-to-five schedule simply does not work for women entrepreneurs. They tend to make up their own rules much more of the time, and are amazing at continuing to have a great impact in the home as a mother and as a partner, while building and leading a business.

The third important point here, if you think about this tremendous dynamic shift happening in the world, is that men have had to adjust to these new ways. Some men are extremely supportive of this massive shift and others just keep "doing life" the old way, and expect it to happen with or without them. We have to be grateful to the men that are welcoming the shift. They are the ones that are the liberal-minded souls that step up to the plate no matter what needs to be done, rather than stay stuck in old traditional rules and ways. These are the men that are flexible, open to change, and able to see the power of each individual contributing in his or her own way in the world. They are supportive in ways that honor the individual women in their lives and the changes happening in the world.

Finally, as a women entrepreneur, we must embrace both our masculine and feminine ways in business. We need both approaches!

Mari Smith (*www.marismith.com*) is a Social Media Business Coach and Relationship Marketing Specialist who was interviewed for this book. She helps independent professionals, entrepreneurs and business owners to accelerate their business profits using an integrated social marketing strategy, with particular focus on Facebook and Twitter. She has great insights about the whole issue of masculine versus feminine traits, especially as it relates to social media: "For many years," she says, "Internet marketing as an industry has been very male dominated. Now that social media has become so prevalent, certainly within the last year, we are starting to build some absolute critical mass. Many women are really starting to step up and be more visible and more successful in this arena because we tend to be relational.

"However, I am careful when I get into gender discussions, because we all have a little bit of both, masculine and feminine. There are some men who are just tremendous at social media because they are very relational and they've also brought the business smarts and the money into it. They are looking at matrix, and they are looking at formulas and systems and the hard numbers and that kind of thing. I think there is a fine balance in using social media if you've got a dominant male Internet marketer type person coming into social media who is very pushy and sales oriented, is not that available, and doesn't respond to his followers. But then if you go to the other extreme, you find those who, male or female, are chatterers. They just appear to be sitting around and chatting all day. And you think, well, why do they make money? What do they do for a living? They've gone a little too heavy on the relational side and they haven't brought in enough of the business savvy.

"I like to really teach my clients and students that you've got to have a blend of both. Everything that I do is strategic and I actually make it look at times like I am just chitchatting. There is a momentary hesitation before I hit the send button or the update button as I ask myself if what I am sending out to the world is responsible. If somebody is upset, am I going to respond in a knee-jerk reaction? Sometimes, the answer is "yes," because, you know, we are all human, but I think that I am just really enjoying seeing this new arena open up that really speaks to leveling the playing fields."

We all know that, for many years now, the number of hours of work considered to be "normal and full time" is 40 hours minimum. In some cases, 40 hours is a joke; it is really 50, 60, or even 70 hours! This amount of time is truly not realistic if one also wants to "have a life." Recently, I had the opportunity to speak with Michael Bungay Stanier, author of *Do More Great Work*. He said it perfectly by commenting that whatever time we specify for work, we fill it, but we fill it with productive time and unproductive time.

What if women business owners started a whole new way – a new workweek that was full-time at 30 hours per week? And what if, in those 30 hours, they were called to no longer do just "good work" but only "great work?" What would be the impact of this in the world? What would be the impact on families?

I speak to women business owners all over the country, and so many are working an incredible number of hours, yet they do not know how to get control over the crazy amount of time spent at work. They become unhealthy, unhappy, and disconnected with family – not the picture of success that anyone really wants. You will find that women leaders limit the number of hours at work. They are more efficient and effective at moving projects forward and, in turn, their impact is bigger in shorter amounts of time. Watching how successful women work is critical to success. They tend to have goals in all areas of their lives, not just business. Having goals in all areas of one's life tends to naturally create more balance.

Very successful women also tend to have a deep connection with family. They have not built their success and lost connection with their families. So, how do they do it? This concept of doing more great work applies to all aspects of our lives, not just the workplace. Connecting conversation happens all the time. There is a lifestyle that the wildly successful women business owner is committed to no matter how big and demanding work becomes. Work is never an excuse for losing connection to family.

Imagine a world where business owners have businesses that are not only successful but are sustainable and do not need their presence so much of the time. Their businesses are based on values versus people. The people they employ work and live within these values. Because of that, there is more flexibility to have a life outside of work that actually feeds the business at the same time. In this world, it seems we'd have less stressed people, more happiness and more grounded children being raised by their parents. *(More on building a sustainable company later in this chapter.)*

Women business owners need to remember that the rules to work by were made for men, and they often do not serve the lifestyle we want. Yet, we have the power to recreate our work world!

Here are some tips from women who have created businesses models based on the 30-hour workweek:

1. Have written and well known company values. The values should be discussed regularly and actually run the company rather than the people.

2. Reduce or eliminate personal use of technology during the workday, i.e. email, cell phone, Twitter, Facebook, etc.

3. Allow work from home and pay by project rather than hourly, *or* reduce full time salary slightly and reward based on quality and bottom line rather than just hourly.

4. Have weekly planning sessions for teams.

5. Be thoughtful about the amount of email that is sent internally. Use face-to-face communication rather than

email for basic communication.

6. Utilize leadership and leader behavior to increase the level of communication among the team.

7. Allow for leaders to emerge at every level of the company. Breed creative thinkers and problem solvers.

8. Negotiate contracts on a workweek that is shorter.

9. Have set contact hours that are less than the ones you actually work.

10. Take vacation often. If you schedule it, it happens!

11. Everyone in the company should have goals in all areas of their lives.

12. Maintain a state of freedom and choice versus the thought that life is all work.

Recently I learned that the Scandinavian nations are evaluating exactly this concept – reducing workweek hours. In an article about the work-life balance in Scandinavian nations, Allister Doyle writes, "While many European workers are fighting to keep working hours from rising and benefits from falling, Norwegians are debating a cut to a 30-hour week from 37 … and have long handed out welfare benefits generous by international standards to help workers balance their jobs with family life." Norway has won the top spot in U.N. surveys as the best place in the world to live for the last five years in a row.

Another area that needs to be addressed here is the amount of time women are spending "wasting time" or in a mode that is anything other than *best self*, which is the only place that we accomplish great work. In the book *Anatomy of Peace*, the Arbinger Foundation discusses the fact that any time we are feeling like a victim, a villain, or even a hero, we are not in our *best self* place, and in that place we are never doing our best work.

That being said, the following are steps to return to our *best self* more quickly. Like an Olympic athlete, the more quickly we return to *best self*, the more quickly we achieve our goals. *Best self* energy is amazingly attractive, rewarding, and successful. As women business owners, we need to be sure that we are allowing nothing to get in our way of being in our genuine *best self* state as much of the time as possible. As emotional beings, this is a very important skill that we need to work on consistently.

In the Big Fish Nation program, we call this recovery: recovering to our *best self*. How do we do this? Following are the simple yet challenging steps:

1. First, just notice that we are not in our *best self* place.

2. Notice what you are: villain, victim, hero, or something else. Ask yourself, what do you need to learn (and/or share) from being here?

3. What do you need to do to get back to *best self*?

4. Now that you are back to *best self*, what do you need to clean up from being in victim, villain or hero mode? (Anything at all?)

5. BE OUR BEST SELVES!!

Obviously, this is easier said and written than done, but know that not being your *best self* costs you money, costs you relationships, and costs you energy. But do not despair! It takes practice, practice, practice – just like any great athlete who works hard to be his or her best at a particular sport. This *best self* topic was included in this chapter because women are such emotional beings, and it is up to us to master our emotions. Men do not respond as women do to conflict and stress. Women tend to allow emotions to affect their day and their energy (not that men do not!). However, we have some work to do, to be better at more consistent mastery of *best self*. Let's do it!

Finally, men have been building sustainable companies for eons and it is about time that women do the same. We tend to build companies that depend on *us* rather than companies that do not. Perhaps we need to be more thoughtful about how to build more sustainable companies that can function better without us!

I remember in 1999, when I was selling my multi-million dollar business, I dreamed that I lost my child; I could not find her in my dream. That same week, I dreamed that the person I left her with did not feed her. Now, mind you, I did not have a child at the time. Women truly take on the persona of being the "mother" to our businesses. However, I *am* a mother now, and I realize how critically important it is to raise a child that can take exceptional care of herself. I realize how important it is for me to raise a child that functions independently yet knows when to ask for help when she needs it. To me, this means building a business that is sustainable *without us*, at least for short amounts of time. This is where the benefits of entrepreneurship begin to arrive.

## MEN – WHAT DO THEY HAVE TO DO WITH IT? EVERYTHING
## QUOTES FROM INTERVIEWS

### Maria Bailey – BSM Media

"My husband has always been my biggest cheerleader. You may find this with a lot of women who are successful in business, but initially it was very hard for me to be the driven one, and I think I had a bigger problem with it than he did. I think we get this feeling like we are going to get married and we're not necessarily going to be the major breadwinner in the family. What I find is that a lot of women, particularly successful women, go through some kind of stage thinking, 'This isn't the way I thought it was going to be. I didn't think I was going to be the breadwinner and why does he get to spend more time with the kids than me?' But then we realize that we are just driven people and we need people to support us and our spouse is the one to do that."

## Alissa Bayer – Milk + Honey Spa

"My husband is my number one consultant, counselor, and confidante. He's been solely responsible for ensuring that we can pay all of our bills and everything else over the past several years, and he's incredibly supportive of the whole thing. …With some of the expansion and things that I am considering right now, he also plays a really good devil's advocate, because I can tend to get really excited and just want to push through and do some of these projects. I want to do my due diligence, and I am very thorough, but he's not afraid to tell me to put on the brakes or rethink things.

## Maureen Borzacchiello – Creative Display Solutions

"My husband's role has been significant. Something he said to me once when I was getting ready to go to the west coast on a business trip really sums up all the time we have been together. I was kind of apprehensive because it was going to be longer than usual; I think it was going to be a five-day trip. My guilt as a mother and as a wife about being gone was starting to pull on my heart a little bit. He just looked at me and he said, 'Babe, just go do what you do so well.' He said, 'Fly, butterfly. Just go fly and spread your wings. We will be here and we will be fine when you come back.' And really, that has always been his attitude."

## Elizabeth Browning – *BeWell.com*/Good Health Media

"I think women are in a better place today than I have seen them in my lifetime. That's because I believe there is a greater understanding of the multiple roles women play and husbands are not chained in by the self-perceptions that those who were fathers in the fifties had.

I think men have been able to create a different vision of who *they* are, and they are not necessarily just the corporate men that our fathers were raised to be. That is freeing to men and also helps women, because men are usually our partners, though not always. There is also greater tolerance for diversity today, whether that's gay or interracial marriage, whatever. There is more tolerance today and more support."

## Lisa Druxman, Stroller Strides

"The reality is that a lot of the business world is made up of male brains. So, I think it's also good to sometimes have a male brain, because my business is so estrogen-based, I can't even tell you. Every client and every employee we have is female! So, for me to sometimes hear a male perspective (from my husband) on something can be very helpful, because our business partners and sponsors are not necessarily women."

## Julie Jumonville – UpSpring Baby

"I was in China for a business trip and Jeff had the flu and he was watching both kids. Grace (who was six then) got up my younger child, got him dressed for pre-school, fed him, then woke up her dad and said, "Dad, I missed the bus. I need you to take me to school." Jeff was in his pajamas because he had the flu and said, 'Grace, just go in and get a tardy slip. Tell them why you are late and go to class.' So, I get an email in China from the principal that says, 'I have to share this with you. Grace came in, said, I need a tardy, because my mom is in China and my dad just can't do it all.'"

## Cynthia McClain-Hill – Strategic Counsel PLC

"I think the most significant thing about my husband is he is very close to his mother and has never really had a view that women and their achievements are less important than men in their achievements. He has taken his own career very seriously and been dedicated to pursuing it, but he has never raised an eyebrow about what I do professionally. He's not overly impressed by it and he's not in any way jealous, competitive, or concerned about it. At one point when I was with the investment bank and our children were small, I actually moved to New York where I was training. So I was in New York five days a week and only back home on the weekends. My husband is the person who got the kids to school and was literally the frontline parent for six or seven months. There wasn't even a conversation about whether that was something he could do, would do, or should do. It was just the way that it was. The conversation was really around whether or not we thought we could make it work as a family and making it work as a family meant, 'Are the kids going to be okay? Do we have everything in place that will make this be okay?' I would say I have never experienced guilt or regret or pressure associated with failing to fulfill my role as a woman in our household. I don't worry about whether I made dinner or he made dinner or whether we bought dinner. …In our house it's just, '*Was* there dinner?' and that's always the focus in how we manage our lives. What are we trying to achieve, and what is the best, most efficient way to achieve it that's going to work for everybody?"

## Sandra Yancey – eWomen Network

"In a business, you can have a great website. You can have fabulous business colors and the other associated marketing collateral. You can have an ideal business plan and a revolutionary business model and, while they are fundamentals, they are not what make success. I am not saying that they are not important. I am saying that they ultimately don't drive success. What drives success is access...and I think the same is true in a marriage. Kym and I, at this particular stage of our lives, have a lot of blessings. We have two healthy kids. We have the pretty house. We have the nice cars, a lot of those things that are nice to have. It helps, don't get me wrong, but it doesn't drive success in our marriage. What drives success in our marriage is access – to being honest with each other, and access to shifting our very low moments. Kym's good at coming to me when I am starting to feel a little bit nervous about something and giving me a hug and saying, 'No matter what, if it all falls apart, we've got each other.' ...So, it's access to each other: our feelings, our fears, and our celebrations in our future."

# CHAPTER 7
## A WAY OF BEING (IN BEST SELF)...
## TO MAKE A BIG SPLASH!

This last chapter of *Splash!* is dedicated to all those in my life with whom I have had challenges being my *best self.* They have been my teachers and have taught me to learn and practice being my best, most powerful self in the challenging moments.

All of us can be our best selves when life is easy and going our way, but those of us who learn to be our best selves in challenging times and with challenging people are those who will create the richness that life has to offer, and will manifest big things in life and in business.

So, let's go! This is the *real* work. Let's roll up our sleeves. This is where our power truly is, and if we give our power away during our challenges, we have given up the ship, so to speak.

This is when we need to dig deep to find our *best self* in all we speak, all we do, and all we are.

In previous chapters, we have talked about how we, as women entrepreneurs, *do* things differently. Yet in all the *doing* of things differently, more deliberately and consciously, we need to be aware of how we are *being* in order to manifest or create big things in the world.

Big things do not happen from a wimpy way of being; big things happen from a strong, confident, knowing way. So often, women come to me and say that they want more self-confidence. However, self-confidence does not come from an external place – from other people or experiences. It comes from within, from how we feel and act. This *way of being* is critical to our success.

## VISION AND BEST SELF

First, as we discussed in Chapter 1, we must look at the big picture, in order to create our *vision*. When we establish a vision and get one hundred percent committed to it, it changes us. Think of someone who is totally committed to something, like an athlete at the top of his or her game. Think about how an Olympic downhill skier, just behind the gate, ready to fly down the mountain, is committed to get to the end as fast as she/he can. Now, think about how that athlete is *being* in that moment. How is she/he *being* when doing the sport? Strong, confident, focused, unstoppable, intense yet relaxed, nimble… we could go on and on describing the way this person is *being*.

As discussed in Chapter 1, the vision we create for our lives and our impact in the world is not set in stone. However, having a vision helps keeps us on a path of movement. While the timeline and details of our vision may change, its essence will not change.

## GOALS AND BEST SELF

Once we have a clear vision as to where we are headed, we need a "North star," a guiding light. *Goals* need to be set, written and decided upon. This was the topic of Chapter 2, which is also where the Goal Wheel was introduced. That same *way of being* we just described needs to be carried over into the goals. But this is where a disconnect tends to happen. We get excited about the *vision*, dive into the *goals* that will get us there, and our energy drops because the results are not exactly what we anticipated. Our *way of being* diminishes and is not as magnetic and magical as it was when we got clear on the vision.

This is when it requires us to become more conscious of our *way of being*, since a lower, heavier energy and way of being will not generate the same results as the other more magnetic, engaging energy. So, it is important for us to focus on the various aspects of our lives that allow us to switch to a *best self way of being*.

This *best self way of being* means being in a place where we are patient, present, confident, focused, powerful, wise, thoughtful, strong, and sometimes even magical. When we are in this place, there is no need to fake it or be anything but authentic.

Sometimes, our words or actions just show up without much thought, and we wonder how we did what we did or said what we said.

So much of the time when we are here in this *best self* place, all is right in our world at that point in time. However, the challenge is to maintain our best selves in the challenging times, so we are able to much more quickly create big things. This *way of being* is critical to our success.

If you think about someone you know who is a success (whatever that means to you), every time you see her you probably perceive her to be in that *best self* place. Life seems easy for her, even in times of challenge. But we all know that life is not that perfect, and it is hard to create a life that constantly has us in that "sweet spot" that we call *best self.* There is always something that challenges that *way of being* and it is easy to be knocked off our *best self.*

## BALANCE AND BEST SELF

So how do we create a balance that is sustainable? The paradox is that, in order to create a life that makes it easy to be our best selves, we need to be more in the *best self place.* Which comes first, the *best self* life or *best self?* As I stated in Chapter 3, *Creating a Full, Balanced Life (Living Fully Today),* "Slow down, be in the moment, and love what you are doing in this moment." When we learn how to be in *best self place*, no matter what, *best self* life shows up. (Of course, there are a few exceptions, now and then; after all, we are still human!) By and large, when we learn to allow *best self* to become more a part of us rather than being dependent on outside experiences and situations, life/success begins to happen with ease.

## INTENTIONS, INTUITION AND BEST SELF

Chapter 4 focused on Intention and Intuition, where we discussed honing this natural skill called intuition that successful women use every day. By noticing, acknowledging and trusting our intuition, we can make decisions effectively and stay in action. This, too, is a part of being in *best self* and noticing things are happening with ease.

A Big Fish that has been part of Big Fish Nation since its inception – my virtual administrator, entrepreneur and friend of 15 years – wanted to have more ease in her life. She set that as her annual intention and, for a one-year period, she focused on being more *at ease* in all areas of her life, and she mastered it! Life, in its own magical way, fell into place – not without issues and snags now and then, but as she mastered this *way of being* at ease, success followed rather quickly!

As you can see from the above example and from all that was covered in Chapter 4 about this topic, *intentions* matter! *Best self* makes life much easier. Our *way of being* impacts our success. This story is a great example of why intentions truly help us create success, both directly and indirectly. Intentions help us with our *way of being* because that is what intentions are – a way in which we become empowered by the choice of being our best selves.

# RESPONSIBILITY, CHOICE, CONFIDENCE
## (AND BEST SELF)

If we are able to see and create a vision that we are committed to reach, and we set goals and intentions to reach toward it, I believe we also have the responsibility to carry out those plans. To me, having a vision is part of being alive. We all have to take full responsibility for making our visions come alive. Our world is a better place when we are working toward living out our visions and, at the same time, working on being our best selves.

I have never seen or heard anyone's vision that was not also good for the world. To everyone who has ever created a Big Fish vision, it is obvious that the world would benefit too, as it is created. That being said, if we are born in this world, I believe that we have the potential to have positive and great impact on the world. Isn't that what every one wants, to have great and positive impact on the world around them?

So, when we are in our *best self place*, how do we feel about responsibility? I venture to guess that when we are in our *best self place*, we are also being more responsible in every aspect of our lives.

*Best self* is easy when life is going well, but what I have come to realize is that the edge successful people have is when life throws them challenges they consciously work to remain in *best self* to tackle the problem.

Think about how challenging it is to stay in *best self* when you are angry, mad, sad, frustrated, afraid, hungry, lost, alone, weak, tired, irritated, or overwhelmed. This is when we most need to practice *best self.* That doesn't mean we must "be nice" and not say what is on our minds, or be less than genuine. Instead, we must notice exactly what it is we are feeling, stay in *best self,* and find a way to communicate our feelings and what we want in a way that honors both ourselves and the other person. While this is much easier said than done, this is truly what mastery of *best self* and being a Big Fish in life is all about.

So just how does one learn the *way to being* in order to create or manifest big things? This is an interesting question, and what I have learned is that the more I think I know how to *be,* the more I realize I have more to learn about how to *be.* (You may want to re-read that sentence again!)

The other thing I know is that the more authentic we are, the more we connect with others, and that is a huge part of being our best selves. The more vulnerable we allow ourselves to be with others helps them feel comfortable with us and truly understand us, therefore making them more attracted to what we are up to. Think of the impact this has on sales and the bottom line.

Leadership over the years has evolved. Great leaders are now more authentic than they have ever been at any time in recent history, even in regard to their presence online. Just recently, I received feedback from someone that my website was not "authentic enough," which I found fascinating as I have been involved in the Web/Internet industry since its inception. Being authentic and vulnerable even counts in this new medium, the Internet. There is a fine line between being professional and being authentic, and being able to successfully merge the two together is where the magic happens!

If you are truly wanting to step into greater success, look at each area of the Goal Wheel (page 38 following Chapter 2 and also at the end of the book, page 148) and ask yourself: How can I be more authentic with those that I touch in each of the slices of the pie?

For example:

- Family and friends
- Your spouse
- Colleagues at work
- Your doctors
- Your exercies friends
- Your financial advisor
- Your kids
- Fill in the blank _____

I am not speaking of being more honest here (not that I am saying you shouldn't be honest) but I am speaking of being more authentic and more in *best self* all at the same time. I'll bet, like me, there are places where doing this is a no-brainer and there are other places in the wheel that challenge you on a regular basis. This is the place where your work is, and like me, I am sure that you also find that some days are easier than others!

There are those days when we find ourselves in anything but *best self place*. I like to call it my "cartoon crazy" place! This is the place where I am saying and doing things that only cartoon characters should be doing. Once you find yourself there, this is a big indicator that it is time to get back on the road to *best self* by working through the following steps:

1. Notice that you are in "Cartoon Crazy" place and STOP!

2. Breathe.

3. As my good friend and Big Fish LuAnn says, "Put on your big girl panties."

4. Ask yourself what you need RIGHT NOW to step into *best self*. Answer the question before you go on. There is always an answer and it is usually simpler than you expect it will be.

5. When you know the answer, reach out for *appropriate* support.

I stress the word *appropriate*, because I know that when I reach out to my friends who love me dearly, after collaborating with them about my problem by expressing irrational, "cartoon crazy" thoughts, the next call could likely be to a divorce attorney, prosecutor or job recruiter! These people love me and want to see me happy, for sure, but they often are not able to help me get back to *best self*. This is why I have such powerful feelings about coaching!

Whoever you choose to reach out to, remember what you are working on mastering is getting back to *best self* in order to do the next big, productive, powerful thing for the sake of your business, relationships, success and your impact in the world. Discuss ways to get back to *best self*. Be authentic and honor the other person and you at the same time. This is the place where, as you master it, every aspect of your life gets lifted to a higher level.

I can share a personal example. Recently, my daughter, who was 4+ at the time, was having one of those moments where something set her off. She was lying on the floor on her back yelling, saying all kinds of things out of anger and frustration. I took a few deep breaths because I knew that if I started interacting with the tantrum (the words, the yelling, the whining) it would be even more of a challenge. I stayed in the room with her and let her know that when she was able to speak with me about what was going on with her, I was ready, willing and able to hear all about it, but I could not communicate with her while she was yelling and whining. About 15 (long) minutes later, she was ready to have a conversation.

I was proud of myself for staying in *best self*, honoring her as a person and her frustration but not her behavior that was, quite frankly, just being bratty! After this incident, I realized that, all too often, I can get caught up in others' words rather than seeing them as just words that come from their place of "being bratty" at the moment – and then I judge that person for it. It was in that moment that I realized that if I can consciously do this with my daughter, I can do this with anyone – if I *choose* to!

Staying in *best self* in challenging situations is no easy task, but it is possible. The more conscious we get about our words, and the harder we work to choose our words carefully, the better we get at this task. I have noticed that successful women are well along on their journey toward mastering this task.

Mastering this *way of being* is powerful! If only the words that came out of our mouths were always authentic, honoring and valuable, we all would be powerhouses – and it is possible! But this *way of being* is not just about words, it is also about our presence, as we talked about at the beginning of the chapter. Remember, the *being* part of this also includes our physical way of being that exists in our bodies and we are in charge of that. Ask yourself, "When am I in *best self?*" and "What does my body feel like?"

Generally, one of the first answers that people give revolves around confidence – so the words only come out when our bodies remain confident, strong, and powerful. It usually is not the other way around, where the words come first, then the body posture. The body has wisdom – the words follow. I highly recommend practicing stepping into the *best self* body posture in places that you tend to allow yourself to shrink. Stay conscious and powerful.

## MEN AND BEST SELF

When I speak of men and *best self,* covered in Chapter 6, I am speaking about how men have had to adjust to the changes in the dynamics of our changing world. We now live in a world where women are stepping into their own power, their own visions, their own needs, and their own impact that they know they can have in the world. When we do this, it has a ripple effect, not one that is good or bad, but a ripple that affects men. Men have had to find a new way, too – a way that honors and respects women as a gender and lifts us up.

Because of how women are having more and more impact in the world, not just in the United States but globally, it is our responsibility to be our *best self* with men in the world, both at home and in the workplace. This is the only way that through all the other areas that I have spoken of – vision, goals, intentions, etc. – we are able to manifest great things, with others, not independently. We are most powerful in interdependent relationships rather than independent relationships.

In order to continue to have big impact and make a big splash, having the support of men in the world truly makes this much more enjoyable and possible. As women entrepreneurs, we are charting new paths to success by embracing both masculine and feminine approaches to business.

## MANIFESTING SUCCESS AND BEST SELF... THROUGH SALES

One area that women have room to get more conscious of, while staying in *best self* mode, is in sales. I find women shrink and step out of *best self* when it comes to sales, yet this is the place that we must stay in *best self.* Confidence sells! Confidence says expert. People want to work with *the expert* in whatever area it is that you work in. So it is crucial to be your best self throughout the sales process. Let's walk through the sales process and talk about staying in *best self* during it.

Women are generally great at having real conversation with potential clients. We are great at supporting women, sending notes and remembering the details of another person. It is such a wonderful important trait we have.

We open up so many doors. We are also generally pretty decent at follow up, but not as good as we can be. Why? I believe the reason why is that follow up is where the real work begins. It is where we have to stand more firmly in being the expert, being our best selves, and walking our talk.

During this phase of the sales process, we have four types of women:

First are those women who love follow up and are great at it. They close lots of sales all the time. They love the challenge of it.

The second group includes those that don't love it but they do it. They tend to have a lower closing ratio than the first group because they tend to step out of *best self.*

The third group does not love follow up but does it, and needs to be conscious about staying in the *best self* or expert place but it is not always comfortable.

Finally, there are those that don't do it consistently and their bottom line represents that. The goal is to have more and more women practicing being in *best self* in the sales process, in order to create better bottom lines.

Our sales bottom lines, obviously, are a direct result of how consistently we are participating in the sales process. One perspective here is that we have a tool that gives us feedback on how we are doing in our sales process – our financials! Get intimate with them. Embrace them! Use them as your *best self* sales feedback tool!

When it comes to the moment of asking the closing question, for some reason we tend *not to do it*! When I ask women why they avoid asking the closing question, I often get such answers as: "I didn't think they would say 'yes.'" "It didn't seem like she was interested." "I emailed but she didn't respond." "I did (ask the closing question) but not in those words." Do you see yourself in any of these answers?

This is the critical moment that we must remain in our *best self* and ask one closing question that only has a yes or no answer, and then stay quiet. Allow the other person to respond. The more genuinely we are in *best self* through this process, the more sales we will make. *Best self* sells!

## A WAY OF BEING IN THE WORLD – OUR TIME IS NOW!

Our way of being in the world – in *best self* – is critical to all aspects of our lives. It directly allows us to create abundance in every aspect of our lives – physically, mentally, emotionally, spiritually, and financially. At the end of our lives, think about the peace we will have as it relates to the amount of time we have spent in that *best self* place, where there are hardly any regrets. *Best self* has us respond with a firm "yes" and a firm "no." In this place, we think and act intelligently and with integrity. In this place, when failures happen (because they do), we handle them with grace and the opportunity to gain wisdom.

Our world is changing. Every single day around the world, women are having more and more impact in the world. On every continent, in every nook and cranny of life, in every industry, in politics, in small business, in corporate America, in third world countries, in the arts, and in the media, women everywhere are choosing to have impact in ways they never have before. We recognize and thank the women on whose shoulders we stand, those who have come before and have demonstrated the way to have big impact in the world. More and more women are choosing to step into opportunities to create big things and contribute to visions made by both men and women, and that is remarkable. It also presents an opportunity for us to do the same.

The opportunity is that no matter if we are men or women, we equally have the right to have visions that we as individuals are responsible for creating and then giving life to. The world is in a state where every great vision needs to be moved forward. Our world needs great visions to come alive and we need the people that own those visions to stand behind them and get in action.

The only way our world gets better is when someone sees a way to make it better, and rather than complaining and moaning, confidently takes that vision out into the world to make it a reality.

My question to you is, "What is the big impact – the 'splash' – that you have the urge to make in the world?" Do you feel that pull? That is the leader in you!

## BE AWARE OF "BACK SPLASH!"

Going for your "splash" in the world can also be a risky thing. I say this because over the years, I have realized that going for your vision, no matter what, can often be perceived as a threat to your closest friends and family. I call this the "back splash" – that place where some around you might feel tugged under with the current you are creating.

Be aware of this, and realize that going for your "splash" in the world is actually a commitment to yourself and nobody else. Sometimes it means letting go of those who are getting in the way of the "splash" that you want to make. Sometimes it means moving forward in ways that were not expected or planned and, if you are focused on your "splash," this could have unintended impact – "back splash!" – on those who feel left behind.

The real opportunity (notice that I said opportunity instead of challenge…) is to remain in *best self,* in order to both make your intended "splash" and not let those whose feelings get hurt or egos get bruised along the way knock you off of *best self.* It is here that you will be able to empathize with those who are affected by your changes, while still standing firm in your "splash." After all, making your "splash" the way you intend takes commitment, focus, bold actions, determination, and daily habits that change the fabric of your life and allow the "splash" to be as impactful as you know it can be.

## WHAT IS THE "SPLASH" YOU WANT TO MAKE?

I invite you to write your vision down, to describe the "splash" that you want to have in the world, and share it with me: *lorin@bigfishnation.com*. Tell me what you need *from yourself* to make it real, for the sake of sharing it and keeping yourself accountable. You and only you are responsible for making your vision a reality. There is nothing like support, but you are the one that sees what you see, and you know what is possible. *Dive in and make your big Splash! The world is waiting and the time is now.*

A WAY OF BEING (IN BEST SELF)…
TO MAKE A BIG SPLASH!
QUOTES FROM INTERVIEWS

### Maria Bailey – BSM Media

"I am all for having a dream board above your desk. I am also all for putting your accomplishments up there. When I created my product line, it was one of those situations where I did a cocktail napkin business plan, and I thought, "Oh, yeah, maybe it'll happen." But I always knew I needed a product line. When I got the first product produced, I put it up on the board above my desk so that when on other days I am thinking, "Hey, that's a crazy idea," or "That's too hard to accomplish," or whatever it is, I can look up at those accomplishments that are on the board and say, "Hey, you know what? Today might be a down day, or it might not be going the way that I want, but look at the things I do accomplish when I put my energy and mind to it." It kind of redirects the energy that I am putting out in The Universe towards successful accomplishments."

## Maureen Borzacchiello – Creative Display Solutions

"One of the most challenging goals we reached was breaking our first million in sales. We had done $350,000 dollars in gross sales in 2005 and at the end of October 2006 we were still only pushing about $680,000. I decided I really wanted to achieve a million dollars in sales that year. We pretty much had two solid months to do this and we had a tiny team and I just rallied them together. I said, you know, we have some really interesting things in the pipeline and I don't know whether they will happen or not. We can't count on that so we really need to roll up our sleeves and dedicate as much of our business day to hitting this goal. You know what, if we don't make it, fine, but I want to hit a million this year. I want to accomplish this and put it behind us and say, yes, we did it! We're so close; I think we can execute it. ...I'll never forget how my husband just looked at me, shook his head, took this really big breath and said 'Amen.' I *knew* we could do it, and on December 22nd, in dribs and drabs, little orders were coming through while all the big chunky ones we were waiting on had not come in yet, but that was the day we hit a million! And on December 23rd, we had $50,000 worth of sales come in. Two deals, 25 grand each, rolled in the day after those that had trickled in!"

## Amy Langer – Oberon

"...we put these projections together and we'd go to our bank or our CPA and others we knew and they would say, 'These projections are crazy! There's no possible way you could do this!' We were thinking, 'Oh, they are so super conservative! We have combed these numbers and we really think we could do them.' And they come back with, 'Okay, we just want to set your expectations, because businesses just don't do this.

They just don't.' Then, my dad comes back and says, 'Well, okay, half the sales, double the expenses, and you might get close.' Come on! We were looking at each other and we think they are crazy. I'll just give you an idea; those supposedly crazy projections put us at $9 million after three years and we were $21 million after three years! We just *knew* we could do more than $9 million! And then, when you hit $21 million, it's not like you had projected $9 million and you hit $9.5. We more than doubled that."

## Sandra Yancey – eWomen Network

"I think that what holds women back is not inequality. What holds women back is a fundamental attitude or belief that what's holding us back is our fear of wild, crazy, fabulous, outrageous, abundant success! I think we are less afraid of failure than we are of success."

# AFTERWORD

It is my intent that this book inspires each reader to become a little more intentional, a little more thoughtful, a little more conscious, and a little more responsible about the "splash" she wants to make in the world. Imagine the ripple effect women entrepreneurs can make around the globe when they take on the challenge!

The ripple effect from that one person influences an unlimited number of other human beings in the world in an unlimited number of ways. This now happens with ease, both globally and locally, thanks to the Internet, social media, television and other forms of mass communication.

When one woman gets more intentional, more thoughtful, more conscious and more responsible for the "splash" she intends to make in the world, the world changes.

What would be possible? I think the better question to ask is what would *not* be possible?

I'd love to hear from you as you set your intentions, make choices, and become fully responsible for creating your "splash." As you do, know that you have other women here rooting you on! Dive In! Make a big splash! Create change – in your world and in the world at large!

• • •

**Facebook:** Lorin Beller Blake and/or Big Fish Nation

**Twitter:** LorinB and/or Big Fish Nation

**LinkedIn:** Lorin Beller Blake

# MEET THE WOMEN BUSINESS OWNERS
## INTERVIEWED FOR SPLASH!

Twenty-one women business owners from across the U.S. were interviewed as *Splash! How Women Entrepreneurs Dive into Success* was written. Quotes from their interviews were included at the end of each chapter, as they shared their experiences and wisdom related to the topics covered. We are proud to introduce you to this diverse group of women through these brief biographical sketches, but invite you to visit the Big Fish Nation website to read their interviews in their entirety. Their stories are amazing and you will benefit from reading about the importance the principles covered in this book have been to their success. Just go to *www.bigfishnation.com/splash* and click on Interviews.

## MARIA BAILEY
### BSM MEDIA

Maria Bailey brings a unique voice to today's moms. She is an award-winning author, radio talk show host, television personality, nationally known speaker and the foremost authority on marketing to moms. Each month she speaks to over 11 million moms on TV, radio, print and online.

Maria is CEO of BSM Media, a full service marketing and media firm that specializes in marketing to mothers. The client list includes Precious Moments, Dell, Avon, Hewlett-Packard, Disney, Cartoon Network, Wal-Mart, Kimberly Clark and many other top 100 global brands. She is an internationally known speaker and has spoken to nearly half of the top 100 consumer brands.

Maria is a six-time author. Her book, *Marketing to Moms: Getting Your Share of the Trillion Dollar Market* (Prima) was the first to examine the buying power of mothers and the most effective marketing initiatives to tap the $2.1 trillion market. In *Trillion Dollar Moms: Marketing to a New Generation of Mothers* (Dearborn), Maria focuses on the emergence of Gen X and Gen Y mothers and compares them to the Boomer mom segment. Her latest book, *Mom 3.0*, examines reaching moms with new technologies, such as blogs, podcasts and social networking. She is the author of *The Ultimate Mom Book* (HCI Books, May 2009).

Maria was the original host of "The Balancing Act" on Lifetime TV and the WE-Women's Entertainment Network for Women and remains a co-host. On radio, Maria is host of "Mom Talk Radio," the first nationally syndicated radio show for moms, and is co-host of "Good Day with Doug Stephan," the #7 ranked morning talk show in America.

Online, Maria is the Founder of *BlueSuitMom.com*, the award-winning Website for executive working mothers and Co-Founder of *Newbaby.com*, the largest resource of online video for moms. Maria's articles can be found in *Orange County Family*, *Mom Magazine* and *Pregnancy Magazine*, among other magazines. She is also the Founder of National Mom's Nite Out. Maria was named one of the most influential moms on the Internet by USA Today, and was among the Power 16 Pack by Nielsen on their list of Top Moms Online. With over 20,000 followers on Twitter, Maria was named to the Top 10 Must Follow Moms on Twitter.

Maria has been a media resource on work/life/family balance, working mothers, marketing, and women business stories for outlets such as the BBC, CNBC, World News Tonight, CNN MONEY, Hearst Publications, *The Wall Street Journal*, *USA Today, Self, Smart Money, Parent, HomeChannel News*, and *Entrepreneur*. She and her company have been featured in *O, The Oprah Magazine, Woman's Day, Money, Chicago Tribune, the New York Times, Wall Street Journal, Miami Herald*, as well as on hundreds of national and local radio and television shows.

She is the proud mother of four and wife to one. In her spare time, she enjoys running, traveling and fishing. She has completed 23 marathons and two ultras.

## ALISSA BAYER
MILK + HONEY

Alissa created milk + honey after completing the MBA program at the University of Texas in 2004 with a focus on entrepreneurship. The original milk + honey spa, located in Austin's downtown 2nd Street District, has been a huge success since it opened its doors in January 2006. A second spa location opened a few years later, closely followed by the launch of SALON by milk + honey, recently named one of the country's top 100 salons by *Elle Magazine*. A second salon opened in July 2010.

Alissa plans to continue growing the milk + honey brand, bringing the concept to a national audience. She is most proud of the amazing team of over 100 enthusiastic and supportive therapists, managers, spa coordinators, and support staff that rally behind her, making milk + honey such an amazing and unique place to work and to patronize.

Prior to moving to Austin, Alissa worked for The Princeton Review for eight years. She started as an instructor while attending George Washington University where she studied English and Philosophy. Her last role at the company was as Executive Director of Operations in New York, before moving to San Francisco to start a private admissions counseling business. Alissa and her husband Shon, a busy software executive at Enspire Learning, work way too much, but enjoy cooking, running around Town Lake and Shoal Creek with their dog, and practicing yoga to help keep them sane.

## MAUREEN BORZACCHIELLO
### CREATIVE DISPLAY SOLUTIONS, INC.

Maureen Borzacchiello, President and CEO, Creative Display Solutions, Inc., has proven to be a skilled executive and visionary entrepreneur during her 15+ year career in the trade show display industry. She and her team provide innovative and seamless exhibit experiences by managing their client's exhibit and face to face marketing programs globally, through production, strategic consulting, design, storage and asset management.

She was appointed to the Customer Advisory Council for American Express OPEN® in 2007. She is on the Board of Directors of Count Me In for Women's Economic Independence and is a Board Member and Chairperson of TSEA NY/NJ (Trade Show Exhibitors Association), among other associations. Awards include the New York State Senate 2008 Woman of Distinction award, the Make Mine a Million $ Business award, Long Island's Top 50 Most Influential Women in Business award and 40 Under 40.

She has been featured on NBC's "The Today Show," "Good Morning America," "Fox Business News," "ABC Viewpoint," "CNBC," *Inc. Magazine, The Wall Street Journal, The New York Times, Newsday, Business Week, Pink Magazine*, and *TheStreet.com*, as well as other business media. Maureen resides in Long Island, New York, with her husband Frank and 8-year old son, Dominick.

## ELIZABETH BROWNING
### GOOD HEALTH MEDIA

Elizabeth Browning is Chief Content Officer, *BeWell.com*/Good Health Media, one of the fastest growing health advertising networks that aggregates more than 38 million unique visitors and 350 million impressions monthly. Good Health Media recently acquired *BeWell.com*, which she founded with Nancy Snyderman, M.D., chief medical editor of NBC News, and Susan Love, M.D, a renowned breast cancer surgeon, researcher and author. She is responsible for overseeing content for all of Good Health Media.

Elizabeth was previously Chief Executive Officer and co-founder of LLuminari, the parent company that launched *BeWell.com*, an online site featuring blogs and commentary from leading health experts on thought-provoking issues, as well as social networking among members. The perspectives of the BeWell experts can also be found in "Live a Little, What the Research Really Says About Living a Pretty Healthy Life," by Drs. Susan Love and Alice Domar.

Prior to founding LLuminari/BeWell, Elizabeth served as President, DuPont Consumer Health, a division of DuPont's Nutrition and Health strategic business unit. During her 20 year career with the DuPont Company, she held a variety of leadership positions and led the globalization of the LYCRA® brand and the company's entry into e-business.

Elizabeth frequently lectures on global marketing and branding. A Harvard Business School alum, she has worked with the Stanford Executive Education Program and the Wharton School of Business at the University of Pennsylvania.

In 2009, she was the recipient of The Strong Smart Bold National Award for Girls Inc. Elizabeth was named the American Heart Association's Love Your Heart Award winner, Go Red For Women Initiative in 2007, and was winner of the Trailblazer Award for The Agenda for Delaware Women in 2006. She was honored by The National Association of Women Business Owners (NAWBO) of Delaware in 2005 as its Business Woman of the Year.

She lives in Wilmington, Delaware, with her family.

## KARA CENAR
PARTNER, BRYAN CAVE, LLP

Kara Cenar has been practicing intellectual property litigation and counseling for over 20 years. Her intellectual property litigation practice has primarily focused on federal and state litigation, pre-trial litigation, and proceedings before the International Trade Commission. She has represented domestic and international companies of all sizes, as well as individuals, in the enforcement of their intellectual property rights and the defense of alleged violations of the intellectual property rights of others.

Kara earned her B.A. and J.D. degrees from Loyola University in Chicago. She is a member of the Chicago Bar Association, the Illinois State Bar Association, and the Chicagoland Chamber of Commerce. She is a Fellow of the Litigation Counsel, a national board member for the National Association of Women Business Owners (NAWBO), June 2009-Present. Past involvement with NAWBO includes serving as Chicago Chapter President, 2005-2006; President Elect, 2004-2005; Advisory Board, 2003-2007; Board of Directors, 2003-2007; and Special Advisor to the President, 2007-2008.

Her civic involvement and distinctions include receiving the Advancement Award for Advancement of Diversity, Chicago High Achievers in 2009; Champion of the Year for Women in

Business – Small Business Administration, Illinois Office and Regional in 2006; and a Charter Lifetime Friend for Boardroom Bound, 2005-2010. She was named to Illinois Super Lawyers in 2010.

Kara and her husband Rick are the parents of three children – 20, 18 and 14. They reside in Chicago.

## MALLIKA CHOPRA
*INTENT.COM*

Mallika Chopra has spent the last ten years working in a variety of capacities in the media world. Her strengths in creating creative content combined with strategic and marketing thinking has allowed her to successfully fuel an entrepreneurial drive in a number of arenas. Mallika is a graduate of Brown University, and has an MBA from the Kellogg Graduate School of Management.

Mallika was a founder and executive at MyPotential Inc., a multi-media company focused on the self-help industry. She was profiled in several publications, including *Forbes, W Magazine, Femina* and the *LA Times*, for her work with My-Potential. Mallika served as one of the first representative for the re-launch of MTV in India, and has also worked with MTV International, Go Network (Disney), and consulted for Yahoo! on marketing and strategic initiatives.

In 2008 she started *Intent.com*, a new trusted wellness destination on the web, to realize her personal intention to connect with others by sharing and listening to each other's stories.

She currently lives in Santa Monica, California, with her husband, Sumant Mandal, and their two daughters, Tara and Leela. She has written two books inspired by them, including *100 Promises to My Baby* and *100 Questions from Her Child*.

# M. MAITLAND DELAND, M.D.
## ONCOLOGICS, INC.

M. Maitland DeLand, M.D. is a radiation oncologist, specializing in the treatment of women's and children's cancer. One of the leaders in her field, she is President, Chief Executive Officer, and Owner of OncoLogics, Inc., a group of clinical cancer practices throughout Louisiana and Mississippi.

After Dr. DeLand received her B.S. and M.D. degrees from the University of Florida, she completed a residency and fellowship in Radiation Oncology at Duke University Medical School in North Carolina. She was awarded an American Cancer Society Clinical Fellowship and is board certified in Therapeutic Radiology. She is also a Fellow of the American College of Radiation Oncology, American College of Radiology and American Society for Laser Medicine.

She served on the 2008 Governor's Healthcare Advisory Committee and is a member of the Health Education Authority of Louisiana (HEAL), an appointment by Governor Bobby Jindal. Dr. DeLand is a clinical faculty member of the Tulane School of Medicine in New Orleans, a Tulane Cancer Center Community Advisory Board member, and an American College of Radiology Physician Surveyor for its Radiation Oncology Practice Accreditation Program.

Dr. DeLand, who has dedicated her career to helping her patients and their families lead balanced and rewarding lives, also serves as a member of the Breastcancer.org Professional Advisory Board.

One of Dr. DeLand's major interests is in quality improvement of medical facilities and the establishment of new programs with medical professionals, specialists, and local hospitals. In January 2008, she opened OncoLogics CentreWomen, the first of its kind in Louisiana, dedicated solely to cancer treatment, renewal and wellness for women. The concept is to treat patients for more than just their oncology needs. Therapy and treatment for the physical, mental, psychological and spiritual needs are addressed with the patient as well. With patients active in the healing process, maintaining each patient's identity as a woman and increasing the quality of life during treatment is the main focus of the center. The goal is to have each woman regain her active identity and focus on a balanced life – work, kids, home and self.

Dr. DeLand takes great pride in offering the most advanced cancer treatments. Through her partnership with recognized physicians and an excellent clinical staff, her philosophy of "treating cancer personally" has earned both Dr. DeLand and her staff the reputation of a facility that not only offers the very best in oncology treatment, but a facility that truly cares for all those they serve. "I love the fact that we have extended families to care for loved ones, which is not always true in large communities," she says. "The support of families and their community of friends and faith are essential to the process of treatment and healing. Just having that kind of support makes a huge difference in outcomes for my patients. Life is short – family and faith are what transcends all medicines."

Dr. DeLand is also a published children's author and has written several book series. *The Great Katie Kate* is a medically based book series aimed at helping children who are diagnosed, or those who have a loved one who has been diagnosed, with serious illnesses. Katie Kate helps to ease a young patient's worries and fears, and helps them to understand their condition. Information about her books and where they are available is available on her website, *DeLandBooks.com*.

## LISA DRUXMAN
### STROLLER STRIDES

Lisa Druxman, M.A., founder of Stroller Strides, is a nationally recognized speaker and author. She is considered an expert in the field of fitness, particularly prenatal and postnatal fitness.

Lisa earned her Master's degree at San Diego State University in psychology with an emphasis in exercise adherence and weight control. She created the weight management program L.E.A.N. Mommy® (Learn Eating Awareness and Nutrition) by Hachette Publishing.

A noted authority on prenatal and postnatal fitness, she has been a presenter at IDEA Health & Fitness Association national and world conferences, and is certified as an instructor, personal trainer, and provider of Continuing Education through the American Council on Exercise (ACE). Lisa was the recipient of the 2007 IDEA Program Director of the Year award and the 2008 Business Owner of the Year Award for the National Association of Women Business Owners.

Lisa was also voted by America as one of "America's Favorite Moms" in NBC's nationally televised contest.

Lisa has received numerous business awards from organizations such as the National Association of Women Business Owners for her unique and successful business. She is the exclusive writer for *Entrepreneur's* new "Mompreneur section" on *entrepreneur.com* and received an APEX journalism award for an article published in a fitness trade journal.

A regular contributor to several San Diego area TV news stations, as well as Fitness Editor to *ePregnancy Magazine*, Druxman has been featured on NBC's "Today Show," CNN, "The Montel Williams Show," "Access Hollywood," and profiled in magazines such as *Entrepreneur, Woman's Day, Good Housekeeping,* and *Self.*

Lisa embraces the Stroller Strides mission statement: "Helping moms make strides in fitness, motherhood, and life." She lives in San Diego with her husband, son and daughter.

## JULIE JUMONVILLE
UPSPRING BABY

When she's not wakeboarding or playing in an all-mom rock band, Julie Jumonville is the co-founder and chief innovation officer of Up-Spring Baby, which develops creative and convenient solutions to improve health, wellness, and safety for parents and young children.

Julie started the company in 2006 after developing Milkscreen, the first-ever home test to screen breast milk for alcohol. With several patents pending to her credit, Julie has since branched out to other products, including Walking Wings, which help teach babies to walk more naturally without the risk of falling, and Shrinkx Hips, a postpartum belt that makes a measurable change in the size of mom's hips.

Julie is an active Board Member for the Mother's Milk Bank in Austin, Texas, was a Profiles in Power winner in 2009, Austin Under 40 Finalist, and serves on AOL's Small Business Board of Directors. Julie and her husband Jeff are the parents of Grace, 10, and Reece, 8. Family is key to her success as an entrepreneur and inventor. Jeff will wear a pink shirt and talk about breast-feeding at any time because he believes in Upspring Baby and its mission. Their son Reece offered to invest in Upspring Baby after he learned that mommy was raising money for the company, and daughter Grace pitched a new product idea called Paranimals that she hopes to develop with her mother one day. UpSpring Baby is truly a family affair.

## LORI KARMEL
### WE TAKE THE CAKE

Did you hear the story about a woman who walks into a bakery to order a cake for her son's birthday and ends up buying the bakery? If so, you've heard of Lori Karmel!

Lori, the owner of We Take The Cake since 2002, admittedly knew nothing about the bakery business, except that she loved the chocolate cream cheese frosting on the cake she bought for her son. A year later, when she was looking for a business to buy, her business broker told her We Take the Cake was for sale and she bought it!

Prior to buying the then-floundering bakery, Lori was a stay-at-home mom and before that had been in the real estate business in Canada. Little did she know that a move to Florida would be life changing, in more ways than one. Two years later, in November 2004, the Ft. Lauderdale, Florida based business was featured on the Oprah show, when We Take the Cake's Key Lime Bundt Cake was chosen as one of Oprah's "favorite things." The show sparked a tsunami of online orders that knocked out her website's server, and propelled Lori's business into the spotlight.

Its gourmet cakes have been featured on The Food Network's "Challenge," "Unwrapped," and "Road Tasted." *InStyle* magazine selected We Take the Cake's prize-winning Chocolate Layer Cake as one of "the best mail order cakes."

In 2009, the company grossed $1.2 million, with about 25 to 30 percent of earnings coming from online sales. A non-traditional bakery in many ways, cakes are baked "to order" only, focusing on customer service and a customized personal touch.

From filling an order for Jamie Fox's 40th birthday cake in 2007, to designing a high-end wedding cake costing $10,000 or more, to baking a little boy's birthday cake like Lori ordered for her son in 2001, We Take the Cake continues to grow and meet the needs of its consumers.

We Take The Cakes' Key Lime Bundt Cake has been featured on the QVC home shopping network. Its gourmet items can be found on-line at *www.wetakethecake.com*, at Field of Flowers stores, and at Aventura Mall in Aventura, Florida.

Lori is a member of the Entrepreneurs' Organization of South Florida, a global organization made up of business owners grossing a minimum of $1 million annually.

She and her husband, Patrick, and 12-year-old son, Sean, continue to enjoy life in Florida.

## AMY LANGER
### SÁLO, OBERON, AND NUMBERWORKS

Amy Langer is co-founder of SÁLO, Oberon, and NumberWorks, three Minneapolis-based staffing firms that have grown to over $48 million in revenue and more than 250 employees in less than eight years. SÁLO and its affiliates are among the fastest-growing contract staffing companies in the country and the top performers in the Minneapolis-St. Paul area.

Amy is active in both the Women Presidents' Organization (WPO) and WomenCorporate Directors. She also serves as President of the Washburn Center for Children Board and participates on the Lake Country School Board.

Most recently, Amy received the 2010 "Forty Under 40" award from the *Minneapolis/St. Paul Business Journal.* In 2009, she was named "Enterprising Women of the Year" by *Enterprising Women.* In 2007 and 2008, Amy earned honors from *Entrepreneur Magazine* and the Women Presidents' Organization as the #1 and #13 fastest growing woman-led business in the U.S. and Canada, respectively. The National Association of Woman Business Owners (NAWBO) also recognized her as the 2008 "Woman Business Owner of the Year."

SÁLO has joined the ranks of *Inc.* magazine's "Inc. 500 List of Fastest Growing Private Companies in America" and has made numerous appearances on the *Business Journal's* "Best Places to Work" list. Further still, Amy and co-founder John Folkestad were named winners of the "2006 Ernst & Young Emerging Business Entrepreneur of the Year Award." SÁLO has also been ranked #3, #13 and #25 on the *Business Journal's* "Fast 50: Fastest Growing Private Companies" in the past three years.

## CYNTHIA MCCLAIN-HILL, ESQ.
### STRATEGIC COUNSEL PLC

As managing partner of Strategic Counsel PLC, Cynthia McClain-Hill leads the firm's regulatory, land use and environmental law practices. Public and private sector clients seek her out for her expert handling of public-private partnership issues and effectiveness before governmental agencies.

Throughout her career, Ms. McClain-Hill has served on a variety of significant public sector boards and regulatory commissions, including the California Coastal Commission, the California Fair Political Practices Commission and the CalEPA Environmental Justice Advisory Working Group. In Southern California, she served on the City of Los Angeles' Community Redevelopment Agency Board, the Small and Local Business Advisory Commission and the Los Angeles Mayor's Economic Advisory Council. She is consistently named one of Southern California's "Super Lawyers" in an annual survey of more than 65,000 of her peers, a distinction reserved for the top five percent of California's practicing attorneys.

A respected authority, Ms. McClain-Hill is frequently featured in a wide range of publications and is interviewed regularly by leading television and radio shows. She is 2008-2009 immediate past-president of the National Association of Women Business Owners (NAWBO) and is past president of the Los Angeles chapter (NAWBO-LA). During the past several years, she has been honored repeatedly for her leadership with business and civic organizations. She received the U.S. Small Business Administration's Women in Business Advocate Award, the 2005 Chapter Public Policy Advocate of the Year Award from NAWBO, the first annual Ruth Standish Baldwin Award from the Greater Sacramento Urban League, and the Thurgood Marshall Award from *Minorities in Business Magazine*. In September 2007, she was featured in *ESSENCE Magazine*.

Ms. McClain-Hill earned her bachelor's degree in political science from the University of California, Los Angeles (UCLA) in 1978, and her juris doctorate from UCLA's School of Law three years later. She was admitted to practice law in the State of California in 1981.

## ORIT
## THE O GROUP

Orit is the "O" of The O Group. And no, she will not reveal her last name unless you are a bank or a customs agent, so you'll have to just enjoy the mystery!

As president and CEO, Orit established The O Group in 1986. It is now one of New York's most successful midsize graphic design firms, one of the few that offers a truly strategic approach. Over the years, she has evolved the company's capabilities and offerings to meet the needs of an ever-changing marketplace. In 2006, after four websites, three locations and too many name variations to count, The O Group celebrated its 20th anniversary and refined its focus: Graphic Design for Luxury Brands.

With a deeply rooted passion for her company and a vision for success, Orit keeps her finger on the pulse of industry trends. She understands the complexities of developing and promoting luxury brands, and her expertise is requested by many, resulting in numerous speaking engagements across the country.

Orit has been recognized for her achievements as an entrepreneur by a variety of associations and organizations. In 2010, the National Association of Women Business Owners New York Chapter (NAWBO-NYC) selected Orit as recipient of its Lifetime Achievement Signature Award. The award is presented annually to honor remarkable businesswomen who have left their unique mark on the business community.

She is the ultimate networker and has a flair for bringing partners, clients and associates together to create brilliant collaborations. Orit's other loves include her son Zackary, husband Paul, retreating to her lake house and designing fabulous gardens, reality TV and of course, Willie, her shih-tzu, who accompanies her to the office every day.

## SUSAN PACKARD
CO-FOUNDER, HGTV;
EXECUTIVE VICE PRESIDENT,
MARTIN FRANKEL
ASSOCIATES

Susan Packard is co-founder and former chief operating officer of HGTV. Packard held a variety of senior positions at Scripps Networks Interactive, (NYSE: SNI), the leading developer of lifestyle-oriented content for television and the Internet. The company's media portfolio includes popular lifestyle television brands HGTV, Food Network, DIY Network, Cooking Channel, country music network Great American Country (GAC) and the Travel Channel.

Most recently, Packard served as President, Brand Outreach, responsible for aligning corporate citizenship activities. She has also served as president of Scripps Networks New Ventures, where she oversaw the development and launch of DIY Network, Fine Living Network, and interactive platforms. Before that, she was president of worldwide distribution for the Scripps cable brands.

In 1980, Susan began her cable career at HBO then moved to NBC to help found CNBC. In 1994 she joined HGTV and became Chief Operating Officer in 1995. Under Packard's helm, HGTV became one of the fastest growing cable networks in television history. Today, HGTV is available in more than 99 million U.S. homes and distributed in 175 countries and territories. Susan helped to build Scripps Networks to a market value of over $7 billion. On July 1, 2010, Susan joined the firm of Martin Frankel Associates (MFA), an advisory group to global business leaders.

Susan has been recognized by industry peers, colleagues, and employees as an innovator, pioneer, role model and mentor. She received the Woman of the Year award by Women in Cable & Telecommunications (WICT) and was profiled in *Modern Visionaries*, a book chronicling the contributions of women to the cable and telecommunications industry. *Contemporary Economics*, a high school textbook, profiled her as an entrepreneur in the field of media specialization. *Cablevision* magazine cited her as one of "12 Most Powerful Women in Cable," and *CableWorld* magazine has repeatedly honored her among "The Most Influential Women in Cable." Susan is the recipient of the YWCA Tribute to Women Award, and in 2008, she was inducted into the Cable Center Hall of Fame. In 2010, she was admitted to The Committee of 200, a select group of global women executives dedicated to inspiring and supporting future women leaders in business.

Packard was the first woman elected to serve on the board of directors of Churchill Downs, Inc. (the Kentucky Derby) in 2004. She served on the board for two terms.

Susan is active in business and community affairs at the national and local levels. She was elected to the Scripps Howard Foundation's Board of Trustees in 2001 and served for six years. She has

served on the University of Tennessee's College of Communication's Board of Advisors. In 2004, she was named a College
of Arts and Sciences Outstanding Alumni at Michigan State
University. She serves on the executive committee of the Denver-
based Cable Center Board of Directors, is vice chair of the board
of an independent collegiate day school, lectures at universities,
and is an advisor on children's healthcare issues and job training
programs for the homeless. In recognition of her outreach work,
she received the E.W. Scripps William Burleigh Award for distinguished community service.

Susan Packard lives in Knoxville, Tennessee, with her husband
and son.

## SHERI SCHMELZER
### JIBBITZ FOUNDER

Sheri Schmelzer is the founder of Jibbitz, which was launched on August 9, 2006, and acquired by Crocs one year later. Jibbitz, the shoe charms she developed, were named from a shortened version of Flibbertyjibbit, a nickname Sheri was given by her husband years ago.

After the acquisition, Sheri retained the title of Chief Design Officer, with the responsibility of overseeing all of the Jibbitz Designs, including all licensed products.

On August 9th, 2008, Sheri and her husband Rich retired and are devoting themselves to raising their children. Both the launch of Jibbitz and their retirement coincided with their wedding anniversary, which in 2010 marked 14 years together.

Their children include two daughters, Alexandra, 12, and Julian, 10, and a son Riley, who is eight. Sheri grew up in Florida and graduated from Lake Highland Preparatory School, then went on to earn a degree in childhood development from Arizona State University. She and her family have made their home in Boulder, Colorado, for the past 20 years.

## KENDRA SCOTT
### KENDRA SCOTT JEWELRY

In 2002, Kendra Scott combined her love for fashion with her creative talents and began her own line of jewelry. Today, the Austin based designs of Kendra Scott Jewelry have found a home in her serene and sophisticated New York city showroom and can be found at top retailers such as Lord & Taylor, Henri Bendel and specialty boutiques around the globe. The line garners the attention of such magazines as *In Style*, *O The Oprah Magazine*, *Town and Country*, *Glamour* and *Life & Style*, all of whom regularly feature Kendra Scott Jewelry.

As Kendra continues to grow her company, she remains committed to the three philosophies that continue to direct its course: family, fashion and philanthropy. Kendra's "family first" philosophy has always been a core value for her growing company. The birth of her two sons during the initial stages of her business influenced Kendra in creating a lifestyle company that is both flexible and fun.

The heart of Kendra Scott's business philosophy is in giving back to her community. Kendra Scott maintains her position on the board of LifeWorks, a non-profit that provides services to homeless and at-risk youth and their families, in Austin, Texas. Kendra is also a co-founder and co-chair of LEAP (Life

Works Entrepreneurs & Professionals), a fundraising and networking organization that connects individuals interested in making a positive impact on the lives of those in need. With her enthusiasm and passion, Kendra is a keynote speaker on the national level for The American Heart Association's Go Red Campaign for Women and is very involved with Dress for Success.

## JENNIFER SMITH
INNOVATIVE OFFICE
SOLUTIONS

Jennifer Smith founded Innovative Office Solutions in June 2001. Innovative Office Solutions provides office supply/furniture products to businesses of all sizes that value a relationship-oriented approach. With a "Relationships Matter" belief system, Innovative's intent was to change what customers can, and should, expect from suppliers. The company quickly became one of the fastest growing multimillion dollar office supply companies in the Midwest.

Jennifer has over 20 years of experience in the office supply industry, including the roles of Vice-President of Operations for U.S. Office Products and owner and President of Town & Country Business Products. Prior to her office supply experience, Jennifer worked in the buying office with the Dayton Hudson Department Store Company for over five years. She graduated with honors from Hamline University in 1989, where she double majored in Business Management and Psychology.

She has been married for 24 years and has two children, ages 16 and 18. She is very active in the community, spending many hours coaching children in track, basketball and is on the fundraising committee for Eastview Hockey. She is also involved with her church community, teaching Sunday school and volunteering time with the Feed My Starving Children organization.

She is involved in many business organizations, including the WPO (Women Presidents Organization), WBENC (Women's Business Enterprise National Council), and the mentor program for the Women Venture Organization. She is currently serving a three-year term on the Dealer Advisory Board of United Stationers.

Jennifer received the Woman on the Way Award from NAWBO (National Association of Women Business Owners) in 2004 and the Woman to Watch award, presented by the Business Journal of Minneapolis, in 2005. In 2010, she won the Enterprising Women of the Year Award in the $10,000,000-$25,000,000 sales category.

Innovative Solutions has been recognized annually since 2001 in the top 25 Furniture and Office Suppliers in the Minneapolis Business Journal and was just named to its Fast 50 list of the fastest growing companies in Minnesota. The company has been included in *Inc.* magazine's Inc. 5000 list of America's fastest-growing private companies in 2007, 2009 and 2010, and was recognized by its buying group, Tri-Mega, for having the "Greatest Dollar Increase in Direct and Wholesale Purchases for 2010."

## MARI SMITH
### RELATIONSHIP MARKETING SPECIALIST

Mari Smith is one of the world's foremost experts on using Facebook as a marketing channel. She is the coauthor of *Facebook Marketing: An Hour A Day* and the lead author of *The Relationship Age*. Dubbed "the Pied Piper of the Online World" by *FastCompany.com*, Mari is a popular Social Media Keynote Speaker, Trainer and Thought Leader.

Mari has a strong ten-year background in the world of relationships and Internet technology, making social media her ideal arena. Through her consulting and training business, Mari helps independent professionals, entrepreneurs and business owners to accelerate their business profits using an integrated social marketing strategy, with particular focus on Facebook and Twitter. After applying Mari's proven social marketing methods, her clients typically experience a significant increase in traffic, subscribers, clients, affiliates, lucrative strategic alliances and targeted media attention. Mari travels the United States and internationally to share her wisdom and provide social media keynotes and in-depth training. She has shared the stage with the likes of Sir Richard Branson, the Dalai Lama, President F.W. de Klerk, Tony Robbins, Dr. Stephen R. Covey, and Paula Abdul.

A self described "bubbly Scottish-Canadian," Mari currently lives in San Diego, California, and has a penchant for turquoise and bling!

## ROMY TAORMINA AND CARLA FALCONE
PSI HEALTH SOLUTIONS, INC.

Romy Taormina and Carla Falcone are Co-Founders of Psi Health Solutions, Inc., the maker of Psi Bands, acupressure wristbands for the relief of nausea due to morning sickness (pregnancy), motion sickness/travel, chemotherapy and anesthesia.

Romy has an in-depth knowledge of marketing with a business degree from California Polytechnic State University, San Luis Obispo. She resides in Pacific Grove, California, with her husband of 14 years and their two sons, ages 10 and eight. Carla has an extensive background in public relations and advertising with a dual degree in journalism and industrial arts from California State University, Fresno. She resides in Seattle, Washington, with her husband of 13 years and their two sons, ages six and three.

Romy and Carla have been nationally recognized as 2009 Trailblazer Awardees from Wells Fargo Bank and the National Association of Women's Business Owners (NAWBO); Make Mine a Million $ Business Awardees from Count Me In and American Express OPEN; StartUpNation's Leading Moms in Business winners; and Intuit's "Love a Local Business" winners. Romy Taormina is the 2009 Woman of the Year from *Woman2Woman Business* magazine and an official blogger for Savor the Success, a national social media network for women entrepreneurs.

## SANDRA YANCEY
E-WOMENNETWORK

Sandra Yancey is an award-winning entrepreneur, international business owner, ABC radio show host, author, movie producer and philanthropist who is dedicated to helping women achieve and succeed. She is the founder & CEO of eWomenNetwork, the #1 resource for connecting and promoting women and their businesses in North America. CNN featured Sandra as an American Hero for her role in mobilizing much-needed resources for the girls' high school basketball team of Pass Christian, Mississippi, in the wake of the Hurricane Katrina devastation.

Sandra is the recipient of numerous business awards including Excellence in Leadership from the Euro-American Women's Council in Athens, Greece; the Entrepreneur Star Award from Microsoft; the Woman Advocate of the Year Award from the Women's Regional Publishing Association; Women Advocate of the Year from *Enterprising Women Magazine*, and most recently, the Distinguished Women's Award from Northwood University.

Sandra is the author of *Relationship Networking: The Art of Turning Contacts Into Connections* and is featured in *Chicken Soup for the Entrepreneur's Soul*, which showcases some of the top entrepreneurs in North America. The inspiring and motivational movie she produced, The GLOW Project, features prominent corporate achievers and successful entrepreneurs who share how they manifest, unleash and expand GLOW to achieve incredible successes (*www.glowproject.org*).

Central to Sandra's commitment to serving others is the eWomen-Network Foundation, a registered 501(c)(3) non-profit that supports the financial and emotional health of women and children in need. Since its inception in 2000, the Foundation has awarded hundreds of thousands of dollars in cash grants, in-kind donations and support to women's nonprofit organizations and emerging female leaders of tomorrow.

Sandra holds a Master of Science degree in Organization Development from American University in Washington, D.C., and a two-year post-graduate certification in "Organization and Systems Development," from the prestigious Gestalt Institute.

Sandra is married and has two children.

# GOAL WHEEL

**Annual Intention**

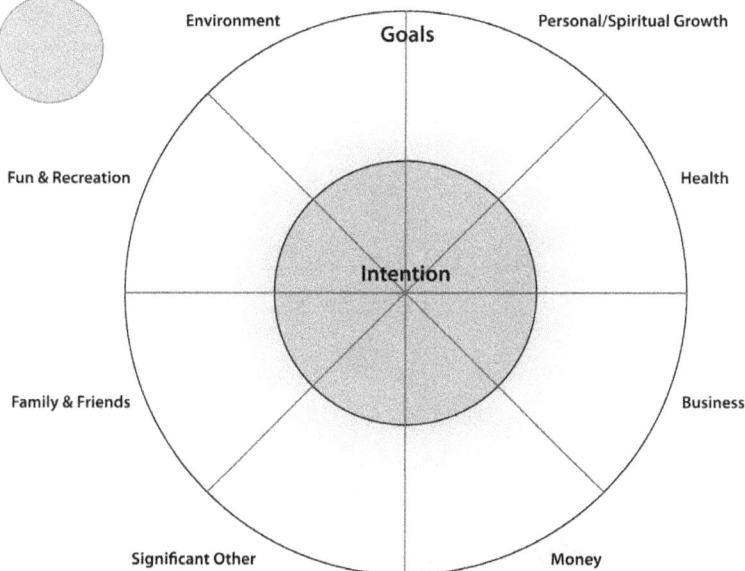

Environment

Goals

Personal/Spiritual Growth

Fun & Recreation

Health

**Intention**

Family & Friends

Business

Significant Other

Money

**Current Year:** _____

## NOTES: _____

_____

_____

_____

_____

_____

_____

_____

_____

_____

## ABOUT THE AUTHOR
### LORIN BELLER BLAKE

Entrepreneur • Speaker • Leader
Coach • Author • Inspirer
San Diego, CA

*Lorin@bigfishnation.com*
*www.lorinbeller.com*
*www.bigfishnation.com*

Lorin's success as an entrepreneur is well proven. In the early 90's, she started a technology company with a partner, built it to a $3,000,000+ firm, then sold it, merging with an entity where, in her role as Vice President of Sales and Marketing, she had the opportunity to sit on the executive team to take the company public in 2000.

In 2001, Lorin left the firm she built and sold to begin working with women business owners. She learned through her success that women *can* have it all but not in the structure of the old work paradigm. It was time to inspire women to mix it up, change the rules, get out of their boxes and re-create success like never before. Lorin became certified as a coach and built a six figure coaching practice in nine months. When she saw that coaching alone was not a powerful enough tool to create the "wild change" she knew women could achieve, she developed a yearlong program, integrating teleclasses with coaching. Along with her team of coaches, Lorin and her company, Big Fish Nation, is having the impact she envisioned – on women, their families and their bottom-lines.

In addition to *SPLASH! How Women Entrepreneurs Dive Into Success*, Lorin is the author of From Entrepreneur to *Big Fish: 7 Principles to Wild Success* (2005) and was a contributing author, along with Steven Covey, to *Roadmap to Success* (2008). Lorin has become very well known within the world of women entrepreneurs as a sought after speaker and inspirer. She has been sharing her unique and powerful perspectives with entrepreneurs across North America for international organizations such as: National Association of Women Business Owners; Canada's Women in Business National Expo; Sales and Marketing International Executives; Young Entrepreneurs Organization; and eWomenNetwork, as well as large Chambers and Associations from coast to coast. Lorin was a co-host on the weekly Kathryn Zox Radio show on Voice America from 2004-2010. Their show was the most listened to show on Voice America Women in 2008.

In 2010, she was the recipient of two Stevie Awards, the world's premier awards for Women in Business, including the Mentor of the Year Award and the Women Helping Women Award.

Lorin's formula for balancing family, a successful career, and volunteering leaves room for fun and adventure. Depending on the season, Lorin may be found hang-gliding onto Stinson Beach in California, horseback riding on a Caribbean beach, skiing in the mountains, wake surfing in a California lake, hiking a mountain somewhere in the world or relaxing in a hammock lakeside in New York's Adirondacks.

Lorin currently resides in San Diego, California, with her husband, Robert, daughter, Sierra, 5, and their dog, Niki, a sweet, blind Shiba Inu.

# ACKNOWLEDGMENTS

To my husband, Robert, for being the inspiration for much of this book's content. Thank you for your patience during the many hours you were alone on the couch while I was writing and committed to my vision. Our journey together has been an evolution, and I am deeply grateful for all that we do with each other and how we learn from each other.

We interviewed 20+ women entrepreneurs for this book and there were so many more that I wanted to interview. Each and every woman that took the time to allow me the gift of an interview had great wisdom to share. Each was vulnerable and allowed us a glimpse into her life, business, successes and real challenges. I am grateful for each and every one of you. Full interviews can be found at: *www.bigfishnation.com/splash*

To the team of Big Fish cohorts: Gail Benmoshe, Amy Cotter, Nancy Duncan and Starla King – thank you! We support as many women entrepreneurs as we do because of you. Because of this team, we advance the vision. I thank you, the world thanks you, and women entrepreneurs thank you!

To all the Big Fish who have been a part of our programs: I learn and am inspired by you every single day. Each of you is making an impact on the world in a grand way. You are changing the ways in which we go about living and playing and working. You inspire me. Thank you for the opportunity to work with you.

To the team that helped make this book a reality: Debbra Dunning Brouillette, Editor; Jordan Campbell, Graphics; Kimberly Maeder, Event Planner; Starla King, Online Expert; Jennifer Maples, Transcriptionist; and Gail Benmosche (our detail professional). It was a long time coming, but we did it! We kept the vision and did a little bit every day. I am in gratitude for all your effort to birth this baby!

To Marci Shimoff: Your willingness to write the Foreword for this book was a dream come true. I appreciate your commitment to women's happiness and love on the planet. Your words of wisdom are deeply appreciated and are such an appropriate way to start this journey.

To my many dear friends: Kim, Jodie, Tricia, and Kathy, who listen to me for countless hours as I process, dream, struggle, take bold action and create new habits. Your friendship and having you to lean on consistently is crucial to my attitude and my success. Thank you.

To my biological family, who has always supported me and my vision, no matter how crazy it was! I am eternally grateful that, as you have followed your vision, you have given me full permission to follow mine.

**Big Fish** NATION

www.ingramcontent.com/pod-product-compliance
Lightning Source LLC
Chambersburg PA
CBHW051829090426

42736CB00011B/1717